FESTIVAL DE FLOR Y CANTO:

AN ANTHOLOGY OF CHICANO LITERATURE

EDITORIAL COMMITTEE

Alurista

F. A. Cervantes

Juan Gómez-Quiñones

Mary Ann Pacheco

Gustavo Segade

PUBLICATION ARRANGEMENTS

Silas Abrego

F. A. Cervantes

Mary Ann Pacheco

University of Southern California Press, Los Angeles

AND

Isabel Castro Berry, Illustrator

All of the basic designs are motifs used in Pre-Columbian Mexico. Except for the cover design, the symbols are found in stamps used to decorate or identify various surfaces and materials.

Cover

Matching profiles of the goddess believed to represent beauty and success provide the basic design elements.

Short Stories

The bird symbol for gods of the heavens is traditionally used to represent the air — governing force of nature.

Poetry

This free-form symbol is believed to derive from a graphic representation of earth and organic life in symmetrical harmony with nature.

Selections from Novels

The never-ending balance between life and death is depicted in the symbol that encompasses both the embryo — life beginnings — and the skull — life ending.

Plays

A natural free-form design represents the balance of fire and water in controlled harmony.

CONTENTS

Contents vii

Selections from Novels

Page

Teatro Presentations

PREFACE

In the Fall of 1973, over fifty "warriors of the pen," as Alurista has described Chicano short story writers, folklorists, poets, and novelists and playwrights, gathered for the most exuberant feast of imagery, color and song yet held in the brief history of Chicano literature. The Festival de Flor y Canto, sponsored by El Centro Chicano in cooperation with the Ethnic Studies Program at the University of Southern California, brought together writers, critics and audience from different parts of the United States for three days to have and enjoy an intense literary experience. During the first two days Chicano authors read their published and unpublished creative works and *teatro* groups performed their *actos* in the evenings. On the final day, literary critics interpreted and evaluated various aspects of Chicano literature, exchanging ideas with each other and with the authors they had reviewed. Through the Festival, not only were the popularly acclaimed Chicano writers acknowledged, but lesser-known writers received recognition and were encouraged to add their works to the growing body of Chicano literature.

Before the Festival, Chicano literature had been a part of Chicano culture only partially examined, even though more and more Chicanos and Chicanas have turned to literature to express both themselves and the movement. Communication among Chicano writers had been largely restricted to literary publications. Hoping to establish a new tie among Chicano literary groups and to extend the presence of Chicano literature, a committee of El Centro Chicano staff, USC Chicano Studies faculty, USC-MECHA students, and interested writers from El Centro Cultural de La Raza in San Diego and the Chicano Studies Center at the University of California at Los Angeles met and formulated the ideas that grew into the Festival de Flor y Canto. The anthology, in turn, grew out of the Festival.

Unfortunately, all the works read at the Festival are not included in the anthology. The editors decided to leave out the critical presentations to allow for the inclusion of as much creative material as possible in the planned volume. Not all the authors of the creative material submitted manuscripts of what they had read. However, all those who did submit manuscripts are represented in the anthology even though space limitations would not permit the inclusion of all the material presented.

The editors, who must inevitably assume responsibility for having decided which pieces were included and which were not, carefully examined each manuscript in an attempt to determine both a representative and a worthwhile selection. No one ideology, theory, philosophy or personal preference dominated the final choices, although the anthology reflects what the editors considered to be the best of each author's work. Our overriding concern is to represent the diversity of Chicano literature as an expression of the diversity of the Chicano people.

Chicano literary expressions are rich and varied in themes, imagery, style and language. If anything, it is heterogeneity that characterizes the literature. Just as there can be no one definition of the "Chicano," so, it seems, there can be no one definition of Chicano literature. Yet both are distinctive and important.

With the second Festival de Flor y Canto having been held in Texas, and the third planned for New Mexico, the editors anticipate that this anthology from the first Festival—the first annual Chicano literary festival—will be a significant part of the unfolding spectrum of Chicano literature. We present *Festival de Flor y Canto: An Anthology of Chicano Literature* and leave it to others to create genres, critical ideas and literary theories.

The editors wish to acknowledge the cooperative work of the many people who made the Festival a reality, the writers who came without remuneration and the many volunteers at USC who coordinated the event so well. For Silas Abrego, director of El Centro Chicano, muchisimas gracias for his long-term support of both the Festival and the publication of this volume. Gracias to those who graciously typed and retyped the manuscript to meet production requirements: María Leyva, Rosa María Cervantes and Marta Rubio. We thank Gary Brower and Teresa McKenna for having read the manuscript and made a number of useful comments. We thank Shelley Lowenkopf for his technical assistance. And to Clarence Anderson goes a special thanks for providing technical assistance and encouragement at various stages.

M.A.P.
F.A.C.

THE AUTHORS

ABELARDO
OSCAR "ZETA" ACOSTA
TERESA PALOMO ACOSTA
ALURISTA
ESTEVAN ARELLANO
RONALD ARIAS
TOMÁS ATENCIO
MANUEL CARO
VIBIANA CHAMBERLIN
JUAN CONTRERAS
VERONICA CUNNINGHAM
NEFTALÍ DE LEÓN
MARCO ANTONIO DOMÍNGUEZ
SERGIO ELIZONDO
RUDY ESPINOSA
DAVID GÓMEZ
JUAN GÓMEZ-QUIÑONES
ALFREDO GONZÁLEZ
JORGE R. GONZÁLEZ
LUIS "LOUIE THE FOOT" GONZÁLEZ
BARBARA HERNÁNDEZ
JUAN FELIPE HERRERA
ROLANDO R. HINOJOSA-S
ELÍAS HRUSKA-CORTÉS
ROSARIO JIMÉNEZ (MATLAL XOCHITL)
ENRIQUE LAMADRID
E. A. MARES
JOSÉ M. MEDINA
JOSÉ MONTOYA
DORINDA MORENO
ALEJANDRO MURGUÍA
PRUDENCIO NAUNGAYAN
ANTONIO G. ORTIZ
HENRY PACHECO
JAVIER PACHECO
TOMÁS RIVERA
LYNNE ROMERO
OMAR SALINAS
RAÚLRSALINAS

RICARDO SÁNCHEZ
SERVIDORES DEL ÁRBOL DE LA VIDA
GUSTAVO SEGADE
FRANK SIFUENTES
MARIO SUÁREZ
MARCELA TRUJILLO
AVELARDO VALDÉZ
ROBERTO VARGAS
PEDRO ORTIZ VÁSQUEZ
TINO VILLANEUEVA
SYLVIA ZARAGOZA

AN INTRODUCTION
TO FLORICANTO

A flower is a moment in a botanical process.
We, in our humanity, have named our favorite moment in
this same process: *Flor*

A song is a moment in the musical process.
We, in our humanity, make it happen with the voice and
other instruments; but it is not the voice nor the other
instruments. It is meaning in sound: *Canto.*

In the condition that we call human life, the stream of consciousness based
upon the analytical perception of matter in flux and that stream of
consciousness based upon the intuition of the permanent human need for
meaning within the flux must be recognized and balanced: *In Xochitl In
Cuicuahtl.* In literary art, words are the things, the historical entities, which
make symbolic meaning through the thought-rhythm of the artist in that
wordless, timeless way we call mythic: *Flowerandsong. Floricanto* happens in
this book as it happens in many books: the works of King David, Sophocles,
Netzahualcoyotl, Shakespeare, Cervantes, Sor Juana, García Lorca, Octavio Paz,
Mao Tse Tung y *tantos otros.* In this book, *Floricanto* happens in a Chicano
way; here are included the prose and the poetry of thirty-five persons who are
the voices of Chicanos and Chicanas, Latinos and Latinas, Hispanos and
Hispanas: *raza, la gente, el pueblo.* These thirty-five voices speak to us from
prisons and schools, fields and factories, individual and collective experiences.
The flowersongs can be as pleasurably exhilarating as E.A. Mares's "Landscape":

> Clouds of ivory hue
> tinge the surface
> of a Spanish sky,
> there to burst and fall
> in Mazarabic light,
> a fountain spray
> beneath an Andaluz sun
> caught in some Alhambran
> garden of my mind.

Or they can sing the clear, clean, bittersweet agony of the *pinto/pachuco* as in
"Sinfonía serrana":

> so
> to nurse both our
> wounds from the
> thorns of deceit

1

> we
> will sign our
> last love-pact
>   in blood
>
>   with
> the scalpel of loneliness
> i'll carve you a sliver
>   of my soul
>
>   to
> paste up in
>   the scrapebook
>   of your heart
>
>   even
>   tho'
>   i
>   know
>
>   poems
> don't bring in
>   much money
>   these days

raulrsalinas
leavenworth penitentiary
1971

Bárbara Hernández voices the discovery of the importance of and the tension inherent in commitment to the collective and to the individual, to the struggle and to herself:

> My soul does not belong to God,
> It belongs to the people!
>
> It belongs to the struggle!
> It belongs to liberation!
> But most important it belongs to me!

What happens in the literature of Chicanos as it appears in this anthology is *Floricanto,* involving a particular dialectic: the Chicano mythic and historical dialectic. In its mythic sense, Chicano literature is general and universal; in its historical and cultural sense, it is specific and unique. There will be those, Chicanos included, who will object vehemently to the very idea of "mythic" reality. Just as vociferously, those for whom "spirit" is ultimate will object to being linked to "base matter." Yet Chicano literature is both myth and matter.

The creation myths of the ancient Mexican and Asian peoples posit an arbitrary moment in space at which the line or dot, which in itself represents pure being, is drawn and reality is separated. At that moment in space, "this" and "that," "here" and "there," "you" and "I" are created. After the first assertion (that of being) is made, the resultant contradictions become assertions or theses. Each thesis must face its own "otherness," its antithesis. Somehow, in the border areas between them, in those areas of conflict where nothing is purely "this" or "that," the syntheses are created. Sometimes a synthesis, one of those border areas, is powerful enough to destroy the elements that created it; oftentimes it is not. Chicano reality is a synthesis which, because it was brought forth as a new entity in the unidentified zone between two world powers, was defined by those world powers as economically and politically powerless. Chicano literature is always, in some way, concerned with this dialectical relationship between a border people and the other two peoples who are, at once, its creators and its antagonists. Wherever national borders have been created, a like people exist. The historical and cultural processes are different, but the basic human relationships, the myths which Chicano artists express through symbols, are essentially the same. Chicano reality and literature continue to relate to that of México and that of the United States, while affirming their own, unique existence.

In the 1960's, the Chicano recognized and asserted his own reality, a reality created by and out of historical fact and as inevitable as any of the essential assertions of the great social entities. Chicano is a synthesized reality that had to be recognized and affirmed by those who were living it. However, one must never forget (or what is worse, attempt to ignore) the commitment that this literature has to the struggle of the wretched of the earth. When the Brown Buffalo, Oscar Zeta Acosta, chooses the cockroach as the symbol that names a reality that Chicanos share with all other cockroach peoples, he is making meaning in a specific, Chicano way and in a general, universal way. *La cucaracha* means many things in México; it means many things in Los Angeles, New York or Peking. Everyone knows, in some experiential manner, that you cannot get rid of cockroaches. But that of the buffalo? The tragic destruction of the earth's most populous herds of large four-footed beasts is known around the world. Equally well-known is the fact that the bison were as numerous as cockroaches. In the two titles, *The Autobiography of the Brown Buffalo* and *The Revolt of the Cockroach People,* Zeta Acosta manages to refer to the tragedy of native America and to the secret joy of knowing that, in the revolution, the cockroach people will avenge the buffalo in all of us.

Can there be moments when the universal mythic situation (its collective relevance) and the specific historical data (the individuality of an event) come together into the truth? It is no wonder that, when Chicanos and Latinos gathered in Denver at the Crusade for Justice Chicano Conference of 1969, they elaborated a *Plan espiritual de Aztlán.* Aztlán springs from the process of history and the process of myth. The Aztlán of the Chicano artist is, like the Troy of Homer, the Macondo of García Márquez, La Mancha of Cervantes, or the Omeyocan and Yollotl of Netzahualcoyotl, a mythic timespace, a symbolic elaboration of a basic human relationship which exists as an ever-potential experience in literature. As literature, Aztlán in all its facets initiates a process each time that symbolic word is experienced within the context of an image or expressed in thought-rhythm, making reference to the dialectical human relationships in which Chicanos find themselves thinking and acting. Alurista, who discovered the symbolic word "Aztlán" and helped add it to the Chicano conceptual vocabulary, was first known as a political activist; yet, he was then, and is now, creating artistically. He structures his thought-rhythm into images with words that can give others insights into a basic human relationship. And so, he writes:

> it is said
> > that Motecuhzoma Ilhuicamina
> sent . . . .
> > an expedition
> looking for the northern
> > > mythical land

wherefrom the Aztecs came
la tierra
de
Aztlán
mythical land for those
who dream of roses and
swallow thorns
or for those who swallow thorns

in powdered milk
feeling guilty about smelling flowers
about looking for Aztlán.
(Alurista, *Nationchild Plumaroja*)

Aztlán, as discovered by the reader upon experiencing the works of such writers as Alurista, E. A. Mares, Teresa Palomo Acosta, Tomás Rivera, Barbara Hernández, Rolando R. Hinojosa-S. and others included in this anthology, is the combination of historical event and mythic relevance.

The process that we call literary art refers to that which is morally good and morally evil, historically accurate and historically inaccurate, politically "correct" and politically "incorrect," for it deals with the whole reality upon which it focuses its critical attention. The artistic process is one way of pointing out the real contradictions which human beings find in life and the need we have to participate in that process is simply too great, too pressing, to be ignored or to be censored. Religious and socio-political Puritans have often attempted to censor art but they could not change the basis for literature's only one "right": the human need for its existence. In 'Las salamandras,' Tomás Rivera makes us experience something of what it is to be powerless: blind and defenseless in an Anglo Caza, like the salamander who, Rivera tells us, is *la muerte original*. Within the context of an image referring to an antagonistic human relationship, we experience the powerless Chicano versus the powerful Anglo and we plumb the depths of powerlessness, discovering and slaughtering the symbolic nadir of powerlessness—the salamander. On another level of human, Chicano experience, in "Turnips and Other Strangers," Elías Hruska-Cortés presents a protagonist who knows, yet hides, his Chicano identity. Jesus Martínez, alias Joe Martin, is hiding from being "Mexican" and the author certainly is not presenting him as a "good" or "sane" man. Hruska-Cortés is exploring the insanity of the Chicano (or anyone else) who runs from his or her past into the plastic nightmare of the present and towards a made future.

Chicano art is, like any art of the twentieth century, surreal and superreal; that is, it is consciously and unconsciously aimed and perceived. Chicano literature, like any literature, helps make us aware of and participants in the dialectics of reality. The Chicano mythic dialectic—the literary dialectic of Chicano writers—is based upon the historical dialectic of the Chicano people and their relationship with Mexican and North American realities. The discovery of the paths and bifurcations within this apparently simple relationship, the discovery of the web of relationships implicit in each of the elements of that relationship, is as staggering as the discovery of a galaxy. The artistic process begins with the people, with the ambient out of which and within which the artist works. Many Chicanos have discovered art within the Chicano movement; many have discovered personal truths about the meaning of art on picket lines, at meetings, and at demonstrations. Chicanos have discovered universal truths and meaning when they were most themselves. Some of them, those included in the present anthology and others, are turning the historical experiences of the struggle into literature. In this way, they are in communication and communion with the people of the world, and other *batos* and *rucas* around this flimsy planet. But, once out of the writer's hands, the work of art belongs to the people. The reader and the critic help to complete the process, to carry it to the infinite number of times that it can initiate the process of the creation of mythic timespace. Aztlán is as real as the United States of North America and México. It is a synthesis of the two, and, simultaneously, an unique reality. Chicano literature, powered by this dialectic, is *Floricanto.*

Gustavo Segade
San Diego, 1974

hort stories

Ronald Arias
Tomás Atencio
Rudy Espinoza
Luis González
Elías Hruska-Cortés
Tomás Rivera
Frank Sifuentes
Mario Suárez
Avelardo Valdéz

RONALD ARIAS

THE INTERVIEW

Buenos días. No, stupid, it's late. *Buenas tardes, Antonio Chávez a sus órdenes.* Smile. *Good afternoon. My name is Tony Chávez and I'm interviewing persons of Mexican descent....*
He mumbled the words, toyed with them rolled them around, bit their edges, mocked them with gestures, raised his voice, deepened it with authority, whispered, lowered it humbly, wiped his brow and wondered if, in this heat, dehydration was worth $2.50 an interview. *Age... sex... marital status... occupation....* While walking through the yellowed, overgrown empty lot, he tried in vain to find some trace of saliva in his mouth. *Religion... Catholic... Protestant...* Other..... Smog clogged the air and his lungs tickled when he breathed. *Where were you born? Where were your parents born?* Nearby, the freeway trucks revved into high gear like giant dentist drills. The noise and heat wrenched his mind from his body, creased it, folded it and let it hang in the air like burnt tissue paper. His hair curled, singed at the ends. *You call yourself Mexican, Mexican American, Chicano, Latino, Hispano, Latin American, Spanish American...? Good afternoon. I'm Tony Chávez and I'm... thirsty.*
Chávez stopped to scratch his ankles; burrs covered his socks. *Have you ever felt discriminated against? No... Seldom... Often....* He raised himself and his head floated somewhere above his shoulders. *What's your usual response?* Fucking heat. Got to do this at night.
The worn dirt path led him past a junked car and a rusty stove with its insides spilled out in the weeds. Looking ahead, he saw two bare chested men on a mattress in the shade of a lopsided tree. Between them was a brown paper bag, twisted at the top. As Chávez approached, the thin man with a snake tattoo on his forearm looked up alertly. "What you got, man?"
Chávez tightened his grip on the notebook.
"You give us forty-five cents?" the older, fat man said. "See?" and he pulled out the empty bottle from the bag. "port costs forty-five cents."
Chávez glanced at the street. The wooden frame houses looked uninhabited. Shades were drawn. A low, fat Impala pointed up a driveway, and a dog lay quietly by a shabby picket fence.
The tattoo came closer. "What's your hurry, ese? Sit down."
"I'm looking for...," Chávez opened his notebook, "Tomás López. You know where he lives?"
"What you want him for?" the fat man said. "You don't look like no cop."
"I'm taking a survey and I want to talk to him."
"Talk to us. A ver, ask me a question. I've got all the answers."
"Leave him alone, Pete. He don't want to talk to no winos. Mira, he's all nervous."
"Hey, you think we're winos?" Pete raised himself slowly.
"I didn't say that."
"But you think we're winos, no?" He held up the bottle, then heaved it into the weeds. "Winos, huh?" For a moment the puffy eyelids closed. Chávez waited, speechless. "Well, that's what we are. ¿Qué no, Jess? Two goddam winos trying to get the feria for a little juice." Pete scrutinized the newcomer. "Hey, man, we ain't going to hurt you. Sit down."
Chávez steadied his voice. "Yeah, okay," and he dropped heavily onto the

7

mattress. The fat man remained standing.

"How 'bout a little wine, man? You lend us something to buy a pint?"

Chávez removed his wallet from his pants pocket and slipped out a dollar bill. "Get me a beer."

Jess reached for a shirt hanging from a low limb and threw it to Pete. "They won't let you in the store without a shirt," Jess explained to Chávez. Pete stretched the T-shirt over his wet belly and walked away.

Facing the freeway Chávez could barely see the hazy outline of the Music Center on the other side. He tried clearing his throat but the phlegm would not rise. Closing his eyes, he felt the dark pit begin to close in. He was walking in circles, and when he fell, the velvet lid or whatever was on top descended softly around his ears. Darkness was heavy, then it spoke.

"Hey, man, you sick?"

Chávez opened his eyes. The clammy hands held his face and the thick smell of alcoholic sweat pricked his nostrils. "What's the matter with you?"

"Huh?" Chávez rubbed his forehead. "I guess it's the sun, too much sun. I'll be all right."

Jess looked at him closely. "You go to school, don't you? That's why you can't take a little pinche sun. Man, you're in poor shape. That's what happens to you school guys. Shit, I used to pull twelve hours in the sun, and all I got was a better sun tan."

Chávez sat up, notebook on is lap. *Macho, brags, likes sun.*

"You got that clean look. But you don't look too sharp now."

"How about if I interview you instead of Tomás López?" *One warm body is as good as the next. To hell with Tomás López. What do they expect for $2.50 an interview, Oscar Lewis?* He put a blank form on top of the small stack of other forms. Ready, get set, and this form along with hundreds of others would be filled, classified, coded, key-punched, run through the computer and finally deposited in neat rows of three-digit numbers—a precise portrait of the true Mexican American. Big deal if Macho Jess subbed for Tomás López. Big deal.

"What do you want to know?"

"Your age." Chávez pushed down the top of his ballpoint pen.

"No! Don't write nothing down."

"But that's not how you do an interview."

"How do I know what you're writing?" Jess grabbed the notebook and closed the cover. "Don't write nothing down."

"If it makes you feel any better, I don't even know your name."

"How do I know you don't? Come on, man. Everybody knows me."

Chávez shrugged. "Okay, but I'm going to write it down anyway, later on. Now give me back the notebook."

"I'll give it back when I'm done. You just listen. I ain't as dumb as you think. Now what do you want me to say?"

"Everything . . . what you do, where you're from. . . ."

"Like I was in the Navy, man. . . ."

Navy veteran.

"I ain't been here all my life. Chale, man. I got in the Navy when I was sixteen. Alright, don't believe me, but I did. They sent me to Oakland and you know what I did? I painted those big ships. Yeah, me . . ."

Occupation: painter.

"I had some good times, man. That's when I got this tattoo. . . ."

Decorated.

"But they kicked me out after I beat some motherfucker over the head with a spray gun. I sprayed him good. He called me a little wetback and I can't take that from no one. So I sprayed him real good. . . ."

Dishonorable discharge.

"When I got back to El Paso, I got married. And that was the wrong thing to do, 'cause my old lady wanted everything. Like she wanted a new car. Man, I couldn't buy no new car. . . ."

Low Income.

"So my compadre and me went out and stole one. And you know what she did? She called the police. Now what kind of wife is that? I was just doing what she said. . . ."

Adjusts well to environment.

"After six months in the bote I was so mad I beat her up good and I never seen her since. That's how I got here. Never went back to El Paso, and I got another old lady. See that house over there? The blue one? That's mine. I painted it myself. And I got four kids. No, five. All of them boys. But they ain't like me. They're going to stay in school and be something. Like you, maybe. . . ."

Five Children.   Encourages education.

"See, you thought I was a bum, puro wino nomás, just sitting on my ass all day. Well, I got a family and a job and this is my day off. What do you say about that. . . ?"

Chávez noticed Pete shuffling toward them at the edge of the lot.

"You got more questions, mister college?"

"A few more, but I can skip it. Here comes my beer."

"No, go on. Ask me a question."

"Okay, are you religious?"

"Man, I was going to be a priest. Te juro, I was that close to being a priest. But I got in the Navy instead. . . ."

Jess saw Pete coming along the path and he stood turning his back to Chávez. An India-ink Virgin of Guadalupe spread herself across Jess' ribs from his shoulder blades to his waist.

Catholic. Devout.

"I had enough for a quart," Pete said excitedly.

"What about my beer?" Chávez demanded.

"What's he saying, Jess?"

"He thinks you forgot his beer."

"Hey, that's right. I did forget. Hey, but don't worry, ese. We'll give you some of our wine. . . ."

"No thanks."

"You don't have to thank us. We didn't give you nothing."

"That's an understatement."

"¿Qué?"

"Never mind."

"Oye, Jess," Pete said, "let's go. The old lady says she's going to call the cops if we don't get out of here."

"Who's that?" Chávez said, looking confused.

"The vieja that lives in that house," and Pete motioned to the blue house. The curtains moved in one of the side windows. "Metichi vieja, she's always after us."

"Isn't that where Jess lives?"

Pete smiled. "What's he been telling you? Shit, he ain't got no old lady."

Chávez looked at Jess. "But you said. . . ."

"I said nothing."

"And the Navy and . . . ?"

"Sure, and my uncle was Pancho Villa."

The two men were leaving when Jess turned around. "Hey, mister college! You know that vato Tomás López? He died two years ago."

Chávez wiped the sweat from around his eyes, picked up the notebook and hobbled out of the shade, following the two laughing figures. "Wait," he yelled hoarsely. "Let me have some wine."

LA CASA DE AQUELLA (por Manito Fresquez)

Ir a la leña no se le escapa a ningún desvelao en el norte si todavía tiene su fogoncito de fierro. El que tiene un trabajito estable, pues tendrá su *fireplace*. Juan hizo su chimenea de piedras relucientes que trajo de las lomas, así con pedacitos de talco y luego con ladrillos verdes haciendo una alacenita para poner sus copas—o *trophies*-de *bowling*, mientras sus padres usan una estufa de leña de aquellas viejitas que tienen un *calentón* para el agua en un lado. A consecuencias, por el otoño e invierno Juan va al monte a traer leña para sus padres, y por supuesto, también para su chimenea. Pero a él no le va mal. Con un medio galón de vino toqué se lleva a Chencho con él.

Chencho se cura, como dice él, y cita a Pacheco: "al nopal lo van a ver nomás cuando tiene tuna." Luego añade él mismo, "Pero no se dan cuenta que el nopal también tiene buen jugo a todo tiempo." Sin embargo, a Chencho le gusta ir al monte. Ese es su jugo. Así nomás escuchan sus cuentecitos, o como dice Pacheco, "las quemadas."

¡Y saca unas pero buenas! A veces hasta le llega a Incocencio y a Fortunato, que si tuvieran estos hombres la herramienta para escribir hasta la Raza hubiera estado escribiendo sus mentiras y vendiéndolas—como los *authors,* ¡eh! Pero Chencho, como sus camaradas, se fue a la leña en lugar de a la escuela. No sabiendo ni leer ni escribir, Chencho platica sus sueños.

J.W. (pa' si no saben, su nombre es John Willie) como siempre anda en busca de cuentos para su profesor de estudios Chicanos, trae a tata Juan siempre con las orejotas paradas buscando cuentos. Y 'hora que trae Juan unas patillas largas, escondiendo sus papalotes que tiene de orejas, y uno de esos bigotes de Pancho Villa, se mira medio apachucado. Niega que parece un pachuco. "Este es el 'stilo 'hora *guys,*" afirma Juan. "Hasta los güeros andan así." De todos modos, muy poco se le está pasando a Juan estos días. A veces hasta Pacheco se admira y dice que algún día le va a cambiar el sobrenombre de Juan Tonto a *Mestro* Juan. Bueno, le queda mejor siendo que es *mestro*.

Pues amigos, este cuento no se le pasó. Y de cierto, algún día J.W. le pasará la quemada a su profesor por un buen *"grade,"* una *A*, sin duda. Despúes escribirá el profesor su librito. "Cuídate," advierte Pacheco, "El que le da pan al perro del vecino, el suyo le ladra." J.W. no entiende. Está todo tapado. Está como aquella gente que admira la tierra pero la siguen vendiendo a los que más los han explotado.

Empieza Chencho su cuento en el camino para el monte en la troquita viejita de Juan. "Isque." Y siempre empieza así, con que "no me tienen que creer a mí, asina me la vendieron a mí," barriendo sus huellas para que no lo pesquen en la mentira.

— Bueno, isque un surhumato vino de México a California buscando trabajo en los ranchos. Después de unos cuantos años, este Fulano, nombrado por sus padrinos en México José Antonio, y con los nombres de su padre y madre Camacho y Barragán (sus camaradas le dijían Tone Camacho) abrió un cafecito con cantina y le llamó *La Casa de Aquélla*. Dijía él que *asina*, cuando le preguntara la vieja al marido que si 'onde había comido que respondiera que en "la casa de aquélla." De aí se volvía un revoltijo en ese estado de matrimonio y el Tone, pícaro como era, se entremetía en el asunto y hacía la de él—era bárbaro.

Creció este negocio. Todos en Califas dijían: "La Casa de Aquélla está de aquéllas." Se destendió el nombre y el negocio por Modesto, Santa María, Sacramento, San José, y hasta pa'l *Mission District* en San Fran y pa' Maravilla en Los. Amontonó tanto dinero José Antonio Camacho Barragán que al fin se compró un lugar en Los Angeles—isque en las lomas de una Bev. Su nombre cambió pa' Joe Bárragan entre los ricos, aí como irlandés. La plebe raza curándose le dijían el Joe Barrigón por panzón que 'ra. Bueno, pues compró buenos carros, aroplanos, pa' ya y pa' ca. Les dió jale a sus camaradas del Valle de San Joaquín, a sus parientes, y a un manito de Nuevo México lo puso a cortar el zacatito. Yo creo que pa 'que no hubiera mitote—"token manito" como dijeran los gringos.

— Apúrate Chencho—le urge Juan. Quizá no quiere que se tome mucho y ya mero llegan al monte, salta y salta la troca en tanto pozo. Como dijera aquel gallo: Pega bien tu troca. Sí, pero en los pozos. Sigue Chencho: — Chuy, el hijo de Barragán por la segunda mjuer—un resultado de la Casa de Aquélla, piloteaba el aroplano—un *Jet*. Joe Bárragan también tenía trabajando como mozas unas Chicanotas pero cueras. Una era nodriza y volaba con Joe en sus viajes a *Washington* a ver a Maclovio. Pues él pasaba muncho de su tiempo en su aroplano pa' no tener que resoyar el aigre malo de Los Angeles. Sufría muncho de los bofes por causa del aigre sucio que cuando le pegaba la tos se sacudía como una máquina de lavar ropa y escapaba de empelotarse. Le dijía el jardinero, el manito de Nuevo México: "Tienes el *tis,* Joe." Lo regañaba Joe Bárragan: "No es *tis*. Es tuberculosis." "Pus eso, eso es lo que tienes. Mi agüela le dijía *tis*," respondía el manito. Al fin se cansaba Joe de su jardinero, pero siempre negaba que estaba asina de enfermo.

Al fin de tanto viaje de Los Angeles a Washington, París, Londres, México, nomás pa' no resoyar las cochinadas de Los, se decidió mudarse de Califas.

"— Oye manito—le pregunta al jardinero—¿Qué no es Nuevo México bueno para aquéllos que sufren de enfermedades de los pulmones?"

"— Oh, el *tis,* dices tú" responde el jardinero.

"— Bueno . . . siiiii y noooo . . . Bueno sí, el *tis.*"

Le dice el jardinero "— O sí. Allá han sanado munchos y hasta se han hecho famosos en la política."

"— ¡De veras! "—mordió Joe.

El jardinero ya se mira de político con el gobernador de Nuevo México. Isque se platicaba solo: "— Que dirá Inocencio y el Fortunato cuando me vean." Y se jalaba un pretal de 'lástico de 'sos que le quedaron de cuando era pachuco. "— Yo tengo un ranchito en la cañada. Aí nos podemos quedar—" le ofrece el jardinero a su patrón.

No gastan tiempo. Se van al aropuerto, se montan en el aroplano como si juera la yegua de mano Nicacio, pero el jardinero le llama *El Águila Negra*. Los dos van tosiendo y escupiendo, con unas carrasperas como tísicos, los ojos llenos de lágrimas por causa del aigre que les quema los ojos—el *smudge,* como le dice el manito. En una hora y media llegan a Alburque. Los papeles los esperan. Hasta los Huesos, un periódico Chicano, anda aí con su *Nikon,* que ni trabaja, queriendo agarrar un retrato. Cámaras relampaguean y reporteros se codean uno al otro pa' hablar con estos dos hombres tan famosos. El papel de la mañana tiene el retrato de José Antonio muy pálido, envuelto en un cute con cuello de zorrío—como dice el manito—y descansando de los hombros del jardinero.

Arriba dice: *J. Antonio C. de Barragán, Mexican American Millionaire Moves to New Mexico.* Aí sigue dijiendo que anda el bato en busca de aigre limpio, pero que se 'spera que recopere y haga pa' Nuevo México lo que han hecho otros tísicos. Viajan pa'l norte al ranchito del manito. Isque en un carro de maya—de 'sos con la rueda en la petaquilla. No creen lo que miran cuando llegan al ranchito. Está lleno de *bosses* viejos, trocas viejas, en trozos de leña, hombres con el cabello hasta la cintura y mujeres que parecen unas monas con el chichero arrastrando. Dice Barragán: "—nos ganaron los gringos otra vez, manito—"

Bueno, C. de Barragán se va pa' Santa Fe en su carro de tinto a un hotel de 'sos nuevos 'onde estaba el barrio del veinte más antes. El jardinero dice: "Yo me quedo con mi carnala en su chantecito aquí en la Cañada."

Sana C. de Barragán. Con su dinero y fama jalla amigos nuevos, también ricos hasta quién sabe 'onde. Dios los hizo y ellos quizás se juntaron. Forman una organización llamada ALAP—Ambiente Limpio y Aigre Puro. Con su fuerza empiezan a cerrar plantas de electricidad, máquinas de rajar madera—las de los vatos ricos que hasta matan las avispas de los rancheros Raza. Ofrecen más pasteo pa' vacas en la floresta, prometen devolver las tierras 'aquéllos que la trabajen, y los de las casitas de cartón que andan haciendo casas nuevas vendiendo gato por liebre, arrancan, cerrando las placitas nuevas.

— Anda Chencho, ya vamos llegando al monte—. le apura Juan.

Seguro que todavía no se le olvida su inversión de un dólar y medio por el medio galón de *toqué* y lo quiere desquitar.

—¿Qué pasó—? pregunta Juan.

— Pus asina pasó, compañero, —dice Chencho. —Le dieron a C. de Barragán un rancho en la floresta. Aí se acabó la promesa pa' los que tenían vacas en la floresta.

Esas placitas nuevas que vemos en un lado del camino, le ofrecieron la mejor placita isque como el tenía una corporación pa' *land development* no tenía que pagar tasación en su dinero. ¡Y tenía tanto! Pus aí ganó. Reglas de los ricos. Hacen dinero sin trabajar. Bueno, el que no brama no mama.

O, se me iba olvidando. Se le apagaron las luces en Los Angeles y todos sus negocios allá se quedaron —conque acostándome con *La Luz* mas que me apaguen la vela. Pero esa luz ni calienta muncho menos alumbra.

— ¿Y qué más? —pregunta Juan.

— Se mirió el Joe, PENDEJO.

— ¿De qué? —pregunta Juan.

— Del *tis,* tonto—Y suelta la risa a carcajadas Chencho.

DIJO PACHECO DE LA QUEMADA: ESTE JUAN SÍ. MÁS SABE UN NECIO PREGUNTAR QUE LO QUE PUEDEN CIEN SABIOS CONTESTAR. QUÉ BÁRBARO, NI PREGUNTAR PUEDE. PODÍA HABER DICHO; ¡DIOS NOS LIBRE DE UN PIOJO RESUCITADO!

Esta es una cábula convertida en fábula.

RUDY ESPINOSA

CACA PEE PEE

Caca Pee Pee is like strawberry ice cream to the Chicano. Its humor, spontaneity has inspired Chicanos to sing of it in corridos, paint of it in murals, and writers to make honest statements as the one above.

Caca Pee Pee has become one of those passwords like Rommel Tank by which the RCAF might single each other out.

Yes, Caca Pee pee is like strawberry ice cream and strawberry ice cream is like wine. It ranges from the meanest Rosé to the grand vintage of a home made wine.

Satan is the man who created Caca Pee Pee. He looks like a man more content to play a guitar and sing corridos to "C" Company on a Sunday than to cope with board members, políticos, committees and pipesmoking intellects who frantically call to order Caca Pee Pee dry-packed and air-freighted to academic toilet departments of higher learning—all in the name of the "Chicano Experience."

But it is this insistent love of good Caca Pee Pee that has made Satan today's living vato, a Chicano boy who grew up during the depression and Eisenhower administration, churning strawberry ice cream for his mother to sell door to door; he now sits at the top of the Satan mine Caca Pee Pee empire, having created the most loose case of Caca Pee Pee that la Raza will have to deal with.

As much sense as there is to loving hand-made tortillas and a hand-made smoke, it is obvious that those who are drawn to what "art of the senses" is left in life will be drawn to Caca Pee Pee.

However, honest pleasures being most difficult to come by, people who know about strawberry ice cream, blue chevys, Tres Flores, Tom Collins, whiskey sours, albóndigas will welcome Caca Pee Pee to México.

May it join the ranks of other good cosas such as a lovely Chicana, a moon México and the music of your stringless guitar that plays within our hearts.

To paraphrase Cuca-Rocha:

"Caca Pee Pee is the root of the Chicano! "

DOÑA TOÑA OF NINETEENTH STREET

Her name was Doña Toña and I can't help but remember the fear I had of the old lady. Maybe it was the way all the younger kids talked about her:

"Ya, man. I saw her out one night and she was pulling some weeds near the railroad tracks and her cat was meowing away like it was ready to fight that big black dog and, man, she looked just like a witch, like the Llorona trying to dig up her children."

"Martin's tellin' everybody that she was dancin' aroun' real slow and singin' some witch songs in her back yard when it was dark and everybody was asleep."

! ! !

Doña Toña was always walking somewhere . . . anywhere . . . even when she had no particular place to go. When she walked, it was as though she were making a great effort because her right leg was kind of funny. It dragged a little and it made her look as if her foot were made of solid metal.

Her face was the color of lightly creamed coffee. The wrinkles around her forehead and eyes were like the rings of a very old tree. They gave her age as being somewhere around seventy-five years old, but as I was to discover later, she was really eighty-nine. Even though her eyes attracted much attention, they always gave way to her mouth. Most of the people that I had observed looking at her directed their gaze at her mouth. Doña Toña had only one tooth to her name and it was the strangest tooth I had ever seen. It was exceptionally long and it stuck out from her upper gum at a forty-five degree angle. What made it even stranger was that it was also twisted. She at one time probably had an overabundance of teeth, until they began to push against each other, twisting themselves, until she had only one last tooth left. It was the toughest of them all, the king of the hill, 'el mero chingón.'

! ! !

Doña Toña was born in 1885 in one of the innumerable little towns of México. The Mexican Revolution of 1910 drove her from her little-town home when she was twenty-seven years old. She escaped the mass bloodshed of the Revolution by crossing the border into the United States and living in countless towns from Los Angeles to Sacramento, where she became the most familiar sight in Barrio Cinco. She was one of the barrio's landmarks; when you saw her, you knew that you were in the barrio. She had been there longer than anyone else and yet no one, except perhaps her daughter María, knew very much about her. Some people said that was the way she wanted it. But as far as I could see, she didn't show signs of wanting to be alone.

! ! !

Whenever Doña Toña caught someone watching her during one of her never-ending strolls, she would stop walking and look at that person head-on. No one could keep staring at her once she had started to stare back. There was something in Doña Toña's stare that could make anybody feel like a child. Her crow-black eyes could hypnotize almost anybody. She could have probably put an owl to sleep with her stare.

! ! !

Doña Toña was Little Feo's grandmother. She lived with her daughter, María, who was Little Feo's mother. All of Little Feo's ten years of life had passed without the outward lovingness that grandmothers are supposed to show. But the reason for it was Little Feo's own choice.

Whenever Little Feo, who was smaller, thinner, and darker than the rest of the barrio ten years olds, was running around with us (Danny, Fat Charlie, Bighead, Joe Nuts, and a few other guys that lived close by) nobody would say anything about his "abuelita." Before, whenever anybody used to make fun of her or use her for the punchline of a joke, Little Feo would get very quiet; his fists would begin to tighten and his face would turn a darker shade as all his blood rushed to his brain. One time when Fat Charlie said something like, "What's black and flies at night? Why . . . It's Feo's granny," Little Feo pounced on him faster than I had ever seen anybody pounce on someone before. Fat Charlie kicked the hell out of Little Feo, but he never cracked another joke like that again, at least not about Doña Toña.

! ! !

Doña Toña was not taken very seriously by very many people until someone in the barrio got sick. Visits to Doctor Herida when someone got sick were common even though few people liked to go to him because he would just look at the patient and then scribble something on a prescription form and tell the sick one to take it next door to McAnaws Pharmacy to have it filled. Herida and the pharmacist had a racket going. When the medicine Herida prescribed didn't have the desired effect, the word was sent out in the barrio that Doña Toña was needed somewhere. Sometimes it was at the Osorio house where Jaime was having trouble breathing or the Canaguas place where what's-her-name was gaining a lot of weight. Regardless of the illness, Doña Toña would always show up, even if she had to drag herself across the barrio to get to where she was needed; and, many times, that's exactly what she did. Once, at the place of need, she did whatever it was she had to and then she left, asking nothing of anyone. Usually, within a short time of her visit-hours (if the illness were a natural one) or a day or two (if it were supernatural)—the patient would show signs of improvement.

Doña Toña was never bothered about not receiving any credit for her efforts.

"You see, comadre, I tol' you the "medicina" would estar' to work."

"Ándale, didn't I tell you that Doctor Herida knew what he was doing."

"I don't know what that stupid old lady thought she was going to accomplish by doing all the hocus-pocus with those useless herbs and plants of hers. Everybody knows that an old witch's magic is no match for a doctor's medicine. That crazy old WITCH."

And that's how it was. Doña Toña didn't seem to mind that they called on her to help them and, after she had done what she could, they proceeded to badmouth her. But that's the way it was and she didn't seem to mind.

! ! !

I remember, perhaps best of all, the time my mother got sick. She was very pale and her whole body was sore. She went to see Doctor Herida and all he did was ask *her* what was wrong and, without even examining her, he prescribed something that she bought at McAnaws. When all the little blue pills were gone, the soreness of her bones and the paleness of her skin remained. Not wanting to go back to Herida's, my mother asked me to go get Doña Toña. I would have never gone to get the old lady, but I had never before seen my mother so sick. So I went.

On the way to Little Feo's house, which was only three blocks from my own, I saw Doña Toña walking towards me. When she was close enough to hear me, I began to speak but she cut me off, saying that she knew my mother was sick and had asked for her. I got a little scared because there was no way that she could have known that my mother had asked for her, yet she knew. My head was bombarded with thoughts that perhaps she might be a witch after all. I had the urge to run away from her but I didn't. I began to think that if she were a witch, why was she always helping people? Witches were bad people. And Doña Toña wasn't. It was at this point that my fear of her disappeared and, in its place, sprouted an intense curiosity.

Doña Toña and I reached my house and we climbed the ten steps that led to the front door. I opened the door and waited for her to step in first, but she motioned with her hand for me to lead the way.

Doña Toña looked like a little moving shadow as we walked through the narrow hallway that ended at my mother's room. Her leg dragged across the old faded linoleum floor making a dull scraping sound. I reached the room and opened the door. My mother was half asleep on the bed as Doña Toña entered. I walked in after her because I wanted to see what kind of magic she was going to have to perform in order to save my mother; but as soon as Doña Toña began taking some candles from her sack, my mother looked at me and told me to go outside to play with the other kids.

I left the room but had no intentions of going outside to play. My mother's bedroom was next to the bathroom and there was a door that connected both of them. The bathroom could be locked only from the inside, so my mother usually left it unlocked in case some unexpected emergency came up. I went into the bathroom and, without turning on the light, looked through the crack of the slightly open door.

My mother was sprawled on the bed, face down. Her night gown was open exposing her shoulder blades and back. Doña Toña melted the bottoms of two candles and then placed one between the shoulder blades and the other at the base of the spine. Doña Toña began to pray as she pinched the area around the candles. Her movements were also imperceptible. The candlelight made her old brown hands shine and her eyes looked like little moons. Doña Toña's voice got louder as her hands moved faster across my mother's back. The words she prayed were indecipherable even with the increase in volume. The scene reminded me of a priest praying in Latin during Mass, asking God to save us from damnation while no one knew what he was saying. The wax from the candles slid down onto my mother's back and shoulder blades, forming what looked like roots. It looked as though there were two trees of wax growing out of her back.

About a half an hour went by before the candles had burned themselves into oblivion, spreading wax all over my mother's back. Doña Toña stopped praying and scraped the wax away. She reached into the sack and pulled out a little baby food jar half-filled with something that resembled lard. She scooped some of the stuff out with her hand and rubbed it over the areas that had been covered by the wax. Next, she took from the sack a coffee can filled with an herb that looked like oregano. She sprinkled the herb over the lard-like substance and began rubbing it into the skin.

When she was almost finished, Doña Toña looked around the room and stared straight into the dark opening of the bathroom. I felt that she knew I was behind the door but I stayed there anyway. She turned back to face my mother, bent down, and whispered something in her ear.

Doña Toña picked up all her paraphernalia and returned it to its place in the sack. As she started to leave, she headed for the bathroom door. The heart in my chest almost exploded before I heard my mother's voice tell Doña Toña that she was leaving through the wrong door.

I hurried from the bathroom and ran through the other rooms in the house so that I could catch Doña Toña to show her the way out. I reached her as she was closing the door to my mother's room and led her to the front of the house. As she was making her way down the stairs I heard her mumble something about "learning the secrets" then she looked up at me and smiled. I couldn't help but smile back because her face looked like a brown jack-o-lantern with only one strange tooth carved into it. Doña Toña turned to walk down the remaining four stairs. I was going to ask her what she had said, but by the time I had the words formed in my mind, she had reached the street and was on her way home.

I went back inside the house and looked in on my mother. She was asleep. I knew that she was going to be all right and that it was not going to be because the "medicina" was beginning to work or because Doctor Herida knew what he was doing.

ELÍAS HRUSKA-CORTÉS

TURNIPS AND OTHER STRANGERS

"Thank God they're gone," he thought, as he turned over in his mind the last episode of their interminable stay. The people from the Centro had made it all sound so positive: two poets to do a three-day workshop at no cost to the school; how could he refuse? Besides, the whole business had the flavor of giving him a certain measure of prestige. After all, no one had ever done this before at Watsonville High.

Watsonville High was not difficult to find; the town was small and the high-school campus was the only area sealed off from the rest of the town by a barbed wire cyclone fence with 'No Trespassing' signs hung at various strategic points along its periphery. The poets had arrived half an hour late, a sure sign of impending disaster in the time-conscious mind of their sponsor, Joe Martin. Joe, whose real name was Jesus Antonio Martínez—a name he detested because it was so foreign-sounding and for which he had never forgiven his parents, thankless un-Americans riddled with poverty and ignorant to the last frijol—Joe was the only teacher of Mexican or Spanish descent at Watsonville High. No one knew his ancestry for sure. His liberal-minded colleagues thought his aquiline features and dark complexion were characteristic of people from southern Spain. The conservatives sought to malign him by accusing him of Mexican ancestry though they were unable to prove it. Others, students and towns-people, had sought enlightenment by questioning neighbors, the police, people in the outlying areas only to find that even his wife, Cathy, was uncertain. She was a blonde from the East Coast and had always thought him to be from Mesopotamia because of his predilection for roast lamb shank. However, his complete mastery of English and his position in the English department had left doubts in her tender mind. Whenever she would question him about his past he would turn red, then white, then blue, then he would squat and turn into a turnip. During their first years of marriage, his transformations lasted only a matter of minutes so that at first she did not notice them, but as time passed he became progressively more sensitive and would stay in that state for hours at a time. She began to take note of this fact and to record it in her diary. Cathy's pleasure in provoking him was related to her vague desire to publish her diary in *MS* magazine as her friend Henrietta had. "There was so much to tell," she thought. But then, one day, while in the super-market shopping, he had embarrassed her by turning into a fifty pound turnip in public so that she was forced to employ the help of another customer to lift him into the shopping cart and to carry him out of the store. Although Joe Martin weighed about 150 pounds, the energy expended in the metamorphosis always resulted in a weight loss which was subsequently regained in retransformation. Joe, however, seemed not always to be aware of these changes. The last time Cathy had dared ask him about his ancestry had resulted in a three-day transformation that almost cost him his life when his mother-in-law, unaware of the strange change, picked him up and was about to slice him and cook him in the turnip soup she was preparing. Fortunately, Cathy had walked into the kitchen just in time to save his life and her mother's anxiety. This had been ten years ago on the first day of a Labor Day weekend. She remembered it well because that was the weekend they had planned to go to Mexico, a place she had read about in travel books and brochures but had never visited. The Monday following, Joe had re-entered the world in time for his 8:00 a.m. class; he had never missed a day and was always punctual. During the course of their married life, Cathy had come to accept certain of his eccentricities though she never approved of them for fear her approval would encourage him to more extreme forms of behavior—something she had always dreaded. And with good reason. His mannerisms manifested themselves differently on specific occasions and reflected varying degrees of emotional intensity. If he was very depressed, he would shrink to the size of a goblin and hide in a shoe or under a cupboard. Otherwise he would pace his study like a peccary. Once, while driving home from a TGIF party, his nose began to turn on and off like a red light with the result that the oncoming traffic became confused and turned into a dance of pirouetting vehicles. On another occasion when he was appointed Temporary Secretary to the Consultant of the Assistant Vice President of the Watsonville Branch of the Council for the Promotion of English as a Native Language in Western Afganistan, he became so exited and elated that when he got home to tell his wife about his good fortune, his words caused feathers to grow on his arms and nape and he developed a flighty attitude to mundane problems for weeks afterwards.

In other respects, Joe was a likeable sort. He was respected by all. His fingernails were well-groomed and always clipped short like his hair. His shoes, always clean and well-polished even on the hottest, dustiest days, reflected the impeccable order he brought with him wherever he went. He had daily affairs with grey ties, his favorite color, which he fastened to his Chinese-laundered shirts with a rhinestone clip his mother-in-law had given him before she was swallowed by a whale on her way to the North Pole in search of the descendant of Moby Dick. Unfortunately, his mood and the color of his tie would change at times in spite of the rhinestone clip and cause an unavoidable and glaring contrast of colors. The day the poets came, Joe's tie showed signs of spotted fever marked with neglect: this was the first time in recent years that he had worn the same tie on two consecutive days. And for the thirteenth time in his history of past events, a nervous feeling scaled down his back like the sudden cold shower one feels at the threshold of momentous events, or so he thought.

Having never seen living poets before, neither in captivity nor in their natural state, he knew not what manner of people they were or, indeed, what species or genus.

That morning he heard a knock at the door and it disturbed him to have to answer before reaching the caesura in the Shakespearean sonnet he had been reading to his class. But his firm conviction that fortune would someday knock at his door drew him away from his immediate audience. For a moment he had forgotten that the poets were due that morning and envisioned, instead, the scattered flight of unicorns across the pampas.

"How do you do?" said the man. "We are the poetas from the Centro. Are you Joe Martin?"

"Oh sure, sure." Suddenly Joe felt his hair growing behind his neck and tried to hide it with his coat to avoid comment and embarrassment. How strange they look he thought. I hope they are not here to make trouble. The man, who looked like Capitán Veneno, may have been Chicano though he had a salty air to him with that halo of seagulls hovering above his head and that Caribbean look in his eyes. The woman looked like a monarch butterfly; she wore a long purple cape that covered her ankles and carried a shepherd's crook in her left hand. "People like these," he thought some more, "are usually those who start riots and commotions. I never should have asked them to come. How I hope they won't start anything that will cost me my job."

"You're 29 minutes 45 seconds late. You may as well go to Mr. Pillbox's second period class in E-3," he directed.

"Where is it at?" they chimed in unison, ". . . where is it at/where is it at/where is it at" through the window and down the hall into the principal's office went the echo until it landed on Miss Larousse's desk and she answered that it was in the second drawer on the left hand side.

"Thank you," said the principal, caught in unpremeditated thought.

"To reach E-3 you go out this door, make a left turn at the second row of lockers, go up two flights of stairs, turn right, go past the first staircase to the second staircase, go down one flight of stairs, turn left, go down three doors, turn right go up thirteen steps and ask the lady in the information booth because I can't give good directions—that's outside my field."

When the poets left they turned right by mistake and walked directly into E-3. Mr. Pillbox was entering the classroom to take roll just as the end-of-recess bell began to ring: it was 8:57 a.m. He later explained that between bells teachers had 4 minutes 53 seconds to get from one class to another and that if you paced yourself right, you could even get a quick cup of coffee and a smoke in the teacher's lounge before proceeding to the next class.

The crisis and Joe Martin's premonition almost arrived, in the figure of Solomón Rivera, on the evening of the second day, and threatened to engulf the land, the ocean, and the status quo if the poets had remained beyond the third day. Fortunately, Solomón Rivera never materialized. Solomón was a Chicano Jew who had come from the Bronx with a repertoire of socialist ideas and who now was the successful proprietor of the most bustling restaurant in the area of Watsonville. His refusal to materialize caused a longing desire to lurk in the brain cells of the poets who had gone to seek him out until the longing was discovered and converted into a sigh of relief by Joe who had sought to avoid Solomón's strange and unconventional ideas and to prevent others from their infection. The mere name of Solomón Rivera would cause Joe to develop an incontrollable twitch in his ears that on severe occasions would give them the appearance of hummingbird wings and would require him to wear earmuffs to school and to give medical explanations for wearing earmuffs on the warmest days. At the last moment Solomón had decided to remain an omnipresent ghost; thus, rendering the crisis invisible. And since Joe believed that what was invisible couldn't hurt you, his spirits began to rise. They rose so steadily and gradually that Joe levitated for six hours before he reached awareness of what was happening. But by this time it was too late; a number of people had seen him and would surely report it to the Board authorities and they would surely fire him for unprofessional conduct and levity.

Joe had not wanted to continue in his family's tradition—his father had been and still was a famous brujo who knew not only how to convert people to stone and to all other kinds of objects and things both of animal and vegetable matter as well as mineral, but also he was one who knew how to control natural phenomena and could make it rain or shine at will; his mother was a curandera from Tegucigalpa known to all as La Chota—Joe had not wanted to follow in the age old tradition because he feared ridicule and what he wanted most was acceptance. Joe had strived hard for entrance into Watsonville society—he had learned to speak impeccable Shakespearean English, had married an American woman, wore Chinese-laundered shirts, ate hot dogs with mustard and drank Coca Cola—and now after all these years he felt as though a malevolent wind had come to blow away the leaves of his cover. And worst of all he was helpless to alter the course of events. Once he had met the poets, he tried to think them away, but they remained to disturb his peace for days. He thought for the third time, all his efforts at avoiding conflict had been in vain; if only he had never invited those poets and yet, in spite of himself, a vague smile marked itself on his countenance. On the morning the poets were to depart, he saw a rainbow from his kitchen window that had the unmistakable signs of his father's art. Now everything had become clear; his parents who had been worried about his disappearance from home fifty years before had finally found him. When he opened the door, his mother, who was also capable of small miracles, greeted him with a light rain that told him his sister, Clotilde, had married El Cuervo, the town priest, and was busy perpetuating the family tradition with her children. Joe had come to realize that he could not escape what he was, and this made him uneasy. Later that afternoon, when the poets came to bid farewell, he was glad to see them go, for he felt the poets had been sent by his parents to spy on him and that the Centro to which they were returning was the Centro de la Tierra from where they had all originated.

LAS SALAMANDRAS

Lo que más recuerdo de aquella noche es lo oscuro de la noche, el lodo, y lo resbaloso de las salamandras. Pero tengo que empezar desde el principio para que puedan comprender todo esto que sentí y también de que al sentirlo comprendí algo que traigo todavía conmigo. Y no lo traigo como recuerdo solamente, sino también como algo que siento todavía.

Todo empezó porque había estado lloviendo por tres semanas y no teníamos trabajo. Se levantó el campamento, digo campamento porque eso parecíamos. Con ese ranchero de minesora habíamos estado esperando ya por tres semanas que se parara el agua, y nada. Luego, vino y nos dijo que mejor nos fuéramos de sus gallineros porque ya se le había echado a perder el betabel. Luego comprendimos yo y mi apá que lo que tenía era miedo de nosotros, de que le fuéramos a robar algo o de que alguien se le enfermara y entonces se tendría él que hacer el responsable. Le dijimos que no teníamos dinero, ni que comer, y ni como regresarnos a Texas, apenas tendríamos con que comprar gasolina para llegarle a Oaklahoma. Y él nomás nos dijo que lo sentía pero quería que nos fuéramos y nos fuimos. Ya para salir se le ablandó el corazón y nos dió dos carpas llenas de telarañas que tenía en la bodega, y una lámpara y kerosín. También le dijo a apá que si nos íbamos rumbo a Crystal Lake en Iowa a lo mejor encontrábamos trabajo en la ranchería que estaba por allí y que a lo mejor no se les había echado a perder el betabel. Y nos fuimos. En los ojos de apá y amá se veía algo original y puro que nunca les había notado. Era como cariño triste. Casi ni hablábamos al ir recorriendo los caminos de graba. La lluvia hablaba ni hablábamos al ir recorriendo los caminos de graba. La lluvia hablaba por nosotros. Y al faltar algunas cuantas millas de llegar a Crystal Lake nos entró el remordimiento. La lluvia que seguía cayendo nos continuaba avisando que seguarmente no podríamos hallar trabajo y así fue. En cada rancho que llegamos nomás nos movían la cabeza desde adentro de la casa, ni nos abrían la puerta para decirnos que no. Entonces me sentía que no era parte ni de apá ni de amá y lo único que existía era el siguiente rancho.

El primer día que estuvimos en el pueblito de Crystal Lake nos fue mal. En un charco se le mojó el alambrado al carro y papá le gastó la batería al carro. Por fin un garage nos hizo el favor de cargarla. Pedimos trabajo en varias partes del pueblito pero luego nos echaron la chota. Papá le explicó que sólo andábamos buscando trabajo pero él nos dijo que no quería húngaros en el pueblo y que nos saliéramos. El dinero ya casi se nos había acabado y nos fuimos. Nos fuimos al oscurecer y paramos el carro a unas tres millas del pueblo y allí vimos el anochecer. La lluvia se venía de vez en cuando. Sentados todos en el carro a la orilla del camino. Hablamos un poco. Estábamos cansados. Estábamos solos. Solos. Solos estábamos. En los ojos de apá y amá veía algo original. Ese día no habíamos comido casi nada para dejar dinero para el siguiente día. Ya apá se veía más triste, aqüitado, creía que no íbamos a encontrar trabajo. Y nos quedamos dormidos sentados en el carro esperando el siguiente día. Casi ni pasaron carros por ese camino de graba durante la noche. En la madrugada desperté y todos estaban dormidos y podía verle los cuerpos y las caras a mi apá, a mi amá y a mis hermanos y no hacían ruido. Eran caras y cuerpos de cera. Me recordaron a la cara de buelito el día que lo sepultamos. Pero no me entró miedo como cuando lo encontré muerto a él en la troca. Yo creo porque sabía que estaban vivos. Y por fin amaneció completamente.

Ese día buscamos trabajo todo el día y nada. Dormimos en la orilla del camino y volví a despertar en la madrugada y volví a ver a mi gente dormida, pero esa madrugada me entró un poco de miedo. No porque se veían como que estaban muertos sino porque ya me empezaba a sentir que no era de ellos.

El día siguiente buscamos trabajo todo el día y nada. Dormimos en la orilla del camino y volví a despertar en la madrugada y volví a ver a mi gente dormida y esa madrugada, la tercera, me dieron ganas de dejarlos a todos porque ya no me sentía que era de ellos.

A medio día paró de llover y nos entró ánimo. Dos horas más tarde encontramos a un ranchero que tenía betabel y a quien, según creía él, no se le había echado a perder la cosecha. Pero no tenía casas ni nada. Nos enseñó los acres de betabel que tenía y todo estaba por debajo del agua, todo enlagunado. Nos dijo que si nos esperábamos hasta que se bajara el agua para ver si no estaba echado a perder, y si estaba bien el betabel, nos pagaría bonos por cada acre que le prepara ramos. Pero no tenía casas ni nada. Nosotros le dijimos que teníamos unas carpas y que si nos dejaba, podríamos sentarlas en su yarda. Pero no quiso. Nos tenía miedo. Nosotros lo que queríamos era estar cerca del agua de beber que era lo necesario y también ya estábamos cansados de dormir sentados, todos entullidos, y claro que queríamos estar debajo de la luz que tenía en la yarda. Pero no quiso y nos dijo que si queríamos trabajar allí, que pusieramos las carpas al pie de la labor de betabel y que esperáramos allí hasta que se bajara el agua. Y pusimos las carpas al pie del fil de betabel y nos pusimos a esperar. Al oscurecer prendimos la lámpara de kerosín en una de las carpas y luego decidimos dormir todos en una sola carpa. Recuerdo que todos nos sentíamos agusto al poder estirar las piernas y el dormirnos fue fácil. Luego lo primero que recuerdo de esa noche y lo que me despertó fue el sentir lo que yo creía que era la mano de uno de mis hermanos y mis propios gritos. Estábamos cubiertos de salamandras que habían salido de lo húmedo de las labores y seguimos gritanto y quitándonos las salamandras del cuerpo. Con la ayuda de la luz de kerosín empezamos a matar las salamandras. De primero nos daba asco porque al aplastarlas les salía como leche del cuerpo y el piso de la carpa se empezó a ver negro y blanco. Se habían metido en todo, dentro de los zapatos, en las colchas, al ver fuera de la carpa con la ayuda de la lámpara se veía todo negro el suelo. Yo realmente sólo las veía como bultitos negros que al aplastarlos les salía leche. Luego parecía que nos estaban invadiendo la carpa, como que querían reclamar el pie de la labor. No sé porque matamos tantas salamandras esa noche, lo fácil hubiera sido subirnos al carro. Ahora que recuerdo, creo que sentíamos nosotros también el deseo de recobrar el pie de la labor, no sé. Sí recuerdo que hasta empezamos a buscar más salamandras para matarlas. Queríamos encontrar más para matar más. Y luego recuerdo me gustaba aluzar con la lámpara y matar despacio a cada salamandra. Sería que les tenía coraje por el susto. Sí me empecé a sentir como que volvía a ser parte de mi apá y de mi amá y de mis hermanos.

Lo que más recuerdo de aquella noche fue lo oscuro de la noche, el soquete, lo resbaloso de las salamandras y lo duro que a veces se ponían antes de que las aplastara. Lo que traigo conmigo todavía es lo que ví y sentí al matar la última y yo creo que por eso recuerdo esa noche de las salamandras. Pesqué a una y la examiné bien con la lámpara, luego le estuve viendo los ojos antes de matarla. Lo que ví y sentí es algo que traigo todavía conmigo, algo puro—la muerte original.

THE BEAN CONTEST DE LA ESCUELA ZAVALA

The overriding mission of Mr. Hilbert, the Zavala Elementary School principal, and of all the Zavala school teachers and staff was to teach English to the almost five-hundred Spanish-speaking Mexican students from East Austin's vecindades. By combining zeal, disciplinary techniques and the rewards of good grades, with iron-clad insistance, the teachers for the most part succeeded in banning Spanish from the activities of the classrooms where the students could be held captive. They could always sit us in the corner with a card tied to a string around our necks and covering our mouths which said; "I will not speak Spanish." Or they could find many other ways to ban Spanish from the class, treating every Spanish word spontaneously spoken in class as a potential curse directed at the teacher presiding over our intellectual well-being. Most teachers took the hard line against Spanish out of love for us, convinced they were sparing us from the cruel fate that came from trying to compete in an English speaking society.

Outside the classrooms, however, whenever groups of us gathered or were in motion in the halls or were enjoying recesses and recreation periods, Spanish continued to be as natural to us as the air we breathed. And teachers were driven out of their minds with frustration when they tried to do something about it, because Spanish not only represented subversive behavior—it represented the failure of the teachers. It made them feel that all their teaching skills and genius inspired pedagogy had failed. They equated the amount of English they had tried to teach us with the Spanish they did not know. They were convinced that they could succeed at instilling English in us by creating in us a revulsion for the Spanish language of our mothers and fathers.

Mr. Hilbert, Mr. Whaley and the more zealous Anglophiles among Zavala school's teaching staff were constantly devising strategies for making Spanish undesirable outside as well as inside classrooms. The constant reminder that "You're in America now, speak American" just didn't sink in since none of us ever doubted to begin with that we were in America. Their goal of ridding us of Spanish was motivated by all that they lived for. Even those who had no inherent dislike for Spanish and the Mexican people, were certain that, if we spoke English during every hour, minute and second of our Zavala school years, then it did not matter how much Spanish we spoke at home, we would grow up to be good English speaking citizens of the Republic of Texas and the United States of America.

The war years did a lot to fan the sparks of the already very alive Americanism. Because we were at war with foreigners who also spoke languages foreign to our English speaking school marms, speaking a foreign tongue became all the more subversive. The Zavala school administration and teaching staff was, for the most, convinced that punishment was only the last resort. They knew enough about motivational psychology and had been influenced by the varying degrees of liberalism and humanitarianism of the thirties. So it became more a matter of finding new techniques and motivations to tame our Spanish-speaking tongue, at least enough to develop a fuller appreciation for English, American's

God-chosen language. It was after all hard enough to teach English to English speakers without the hindrance of another language.

One semester, the Zavala school administration and staff devised a scheme, an elaborate game which seemed to have all the elements required to discourage Mexican children from speaking Spanish by encouraging them to speak English. Knowing how much Mexicans loved beans, they invented a bean game for us. All the teachers were supplied with quantities of beans and a number of Bull Durham bags (empty of tobacco of course) and the rules of the game were given. The object of the game was to take a bean from a classmate who could not restrain himself or herself from uttering words in Spanish. We naturally got all excited about the game, enjoying the novelty of the Bull Durham bags richly filled with beans. Some of us took the game very seriously, because at the end of the week the best bean hoarders would be rewarded with an abundance of red and blue stars and a certificate of excellence with a red and blue ribbon attached to a gold seal.

When the game first started, silence filled the halls because we could not trust our own tongues. The more Anglocized students suddenly decided to stick close to the students with the largest Spanish vocabularies. Those who spoke practically no English at all were forced to commit themselves to silence. Some students spent hours exchanging beans, amazing themselves because they would end-up more or less with the same amount of beans they started out with.

Soon all kinds of interesting conversations could be heard.

"I heard you . . . you said ball in Spanish. Give me a bean." shouted Víctor Sánchez to Mike Arredondo.

"Mentiras!" responded Mike.

"You said 'mentiras,' you owe me another bean!"

"But you said 'mentiras' too, so I don't owe you a bean for that!"

"Yea, but you said 'mentiras' twice!"

And another time two other students got into it.

"I heard you! I heard you!"

"Heard what?"

"Tú sabes . . . I mean you."

"Ha! Ha! Ha!"

" ¡Cabrón!"

"I'm going to tell the teacher you called me 'cabrón'."

Zas . . . Zas

"Le voy a decir a mi hermano que me pegaste!"

By the third day chaos had broken loose. Arguments and fights erupted everywhere. But those with good natures and a sense of humor gave their beans away willingly, glad to demonstrate que no eran angabachados. Some pooled their beans with their closest friends and took them home to cook. Others got the enterprising idea of planting their beans on the side of the school building, inspired no doubt by the story of Jack and the Beanstalk and feeling justified that, with a good crop, they would win the contest. Others raided the bean bags in their own home and smuggled beans into school. When the teachers saw how much disruption the game was causing and how much fun we were having catching each other using Spanish, they realized their mistake. They realized that it was the Spanish language that was motivating our urge for rewards. They realized also that our ears were developing a sharper sensitivity for Spanish.

Besides, by the fourth day it was evident that there was no one willing to come forth to claim the prizes and awards. No one felt ahead. So they dropped the game and confiscated the bean bags. And when the crop of beans on the side of the school became evident, the school janitor was ordered to attack it with a hoe, dashing the dreams of bean stalks at Zavala school.

MARIO SUÁREZ

LOS COYOTES

In *El Hoyo,* when an individual devotes himself to arranging the immigration status of others, he is referred to as a *coyote.* Everybody knows that the immigration business, la *'migra,'* is full of opportunities for graft and outright blackmail. If an individual is a farm labor contractor he is also a *coyote.* Delivering the hungry and the desperate to known degradation and exploitation, how could he be anything but? In fact, if an individual works with a pencil . . . But why go on? *Coyotes* insist that there is *coyotada* right down the line to the pick and shovel.

Many years ago, during a depression which reduced many a *coyote* to work the streets selling lost treasure maps, a massive individual named Casimiro Ancheta arrived in El Hoyo. Because of his striking appearance, Casimiro was soon able to win the hand of Agripina, a working widow whose large family refused to accept him as a step-father and then persisted, long after a quick marriage, to insult him, to question his character, to threaten him, and to make remarks about his appetite. Casimiro smarted under the constant barrage of insults, threats, and remarks but stood his ground. After all, Casimiro said in his defense, he was a general in the Mexican army. He was waiting for the true Mexican revolution to vindicate him as soon as the traitors and torturers of Mexican Liberty who now had the upper hand were overthrown. Then he would go back to Mexico to resume his command, back to his homes and lands, back to his . . . Naturally, he would take Agripina with him.

Meanwhile having little to do, it did not take Casimiro Ancheta very long to meet and become the friend of Pancho Pérez, a thin, moribund appearing individual who had made his front room into an office and hung out a sign—Notary. However, since being a notary was neither remunerative nor time consuming, Pancho was also in the *reina business,* that of electing queens for the Sixteenth of September and the Fifth of May, Mexico's two most glorious national holidays.

Whenever Casimiro dropped by his friend Pancho's office, by the time he had his numerous cups of coffee and wiped clean a couple of plates of *pan dulce,* sweet bread, the conversation ultimately led to the subject of oppression, on both sides of the border. "Damn, Pancho, how I hate the cursed *coyotes* who thrive on our beloved, long suffering race. Always they are sucking the blood of the weak and the trusting, disregarding all morality and justice. Just the other day I saw Anacleto Moreno putting on the airs of a decent man when everybody knows the foul source of his wealth."

"Alas, my esteemed Casimiro, what you say is tragic but true. The world seems to only applaud insincerity and false appearances. Truth and justice are dead," said Pancho, gazing sadly at a picture of Benito Juárez framed on one wall and then at a picture of Porfirio Díaz framed on the other.

"Still, Pancho, I will never allow such a sad state of affairs to defeat me. There will come a day when the forces of truth and justice will carry the day," said Casimiro, reaching for the last piece of sweet bread in the plate in front of him. "Great forces."

Whether the forces which gathered all over the world and those which rose to oppose them stood for truth and justice is a matter of geography. However, after the Imperial Navy bombed Pearl Harbor, El Hoyo's fathers and sons flocked to the colors, some drawn by posters and others ensnared by the local draft board. In addition, a war plant to make bombers was set up and an air base mushroomed in the desert to train pilots and crews. In the ensuing labor scarcity even Casimiro and Pancho found jobs standing behind a supply window checking out tools at the war plant.

Now, while Pancho Pérez might have been satisfied with the novelty of a constant paycheck and be content to check out tools for the duration of the war, such was not the case with Casimiro Ancheta. From the check out window Casimiro could not help but notice, and not without envy, the numerous raffles, lotteries, and pools going on before his very eyes. It was then that his feet began to hurt. In fact, on hearing of shortages, rationing, hoarding, and then thinking of the logical speculation, Casimiro's feet not only hurt but the pains shot up his legs, his spine. Thus Casimiro knew the opportune moment for helping his beloved, long suffering race had arrived. He said to Pancho, "The moment has arrived, firm comrade, when we must start to fight for El Hoyo's heroes on the home front. We must organize in order to help our race to have the true representation it justly deserves. Only that way can we guarantee all our heroes a job as well as unlimited opportunities when they return from the fields of battle."

"Well said," responded Pancho. "But how?"

"By starting an organization, my esteemed, an organization we can hand over to our heroes when they return. That is my dream."

The plan set, for a whole week Casimiro and Pancho went about El Hoyo inviting every Christian wife and mother to attend the initial meeting. And, the sincerity of their plea was so touching that Pancho's office, bedrooms, kitchen, and back yard proved small for the crowd. Then Pancho, calling for everyone's attention, welcomed the assembled and introduced Casimiro Ancheta, whose brilliant idea had brought them together. The latter got up and after thanking Pancho Pérez, outlined his proposal for bringing civil light and political prestige to El Hoyo. In a long and impassioned speech ringing with the words faith, trust, unity, and strength, Casimiro, choking with emotion, beseeched the assembled wives and mothers for support. It was the only way, he assured them, of attaining political power and economic security for El Hoyo's husbands and sons fighting abroad. When Casimiro was through, the assembled wives and mothers clapped and cheered. And that very night the Alliance of Mexican-American Christian Wives and Mothers was formed, with Casimiro Ancheta and Pancho Pérez, naturally, being named president and vice president by acclamation.

In a short time, so great did the burdens of office become that Casimiro and Pancho left their jobs at the war plant to dedicate themselves body and soul to their mission. At meetings Casimiro and Pancho constantly assured the wives and mothers that that very morning special letters had been sent to General MacArthur and General Eisenhower personally, asking them to take good care of El Hoyo's fathers and sons. When an allotment check failed to arrive in time, it was always Pancho Pérez who looked into the matter. When a promotion was given or a leave was granted, Casimiro's great influence was no doubt responsible. So trusted did Casimiro and Pancho become that contributions, dues, and assessments were unflinchingly given by the Alliance of Mexican-American Christian Wives and Mothers for everything from building a clubhouse for the returning heroes to saying masses for the unfortunate ones who remained buried in far away battlefields or returned in caskets. So great did Casimiro and Pancho come to loom in the lives of the Alliance wives and mothers that more than one found herself looking into the faces of Casimiro and Pancho with moist eyes and saying, "I will light a candle for each of you."

All of this dedication, naturally, was not without its rewards. Casimiro Ancheta, like a true general, was seen everywhere squiring manicured and perfumed *mosquitas muertas* from Mexico which he promptly introduced as his nieces. Pancho Pérez, in turn, bought a fashionable house in the east side of town where chicanos were normally excluded and in all circumstances whispered about. And, being the guests of honor at so many testimonials, the politicians could not fail but take notice and, for fear of retribution at the polls, made sure that Casimiro and Pancho were present at all public functions, representing, naturally, the interests of the Alliance of Mexican-American Christian Wives and Mothers. Then came the bombs on Hiroshima and Nagasaki. . . .

When the returning husbands and sons found out their allotment checks and money orders had been disappearing in the form of contributions, dues, quotas, and assessments, they shouted angrily, "Get out of that silly club." Others said, "Can't you see that those two are nothing but a pair of swindlers?" And still others simply said, "Those two coyotes really found themselves a nest of suckers." When the rumors of dissatisfaction reached Casimiro and Pancho's ears, they shrugged them off as *celitos,* jealousy. When vile insults about their ancestry were shouted at them, Casimiro and Pancho muttered, "Bolsheviks."

In no time at all the membership of the Alliance of Mexican-American Christian Wives and Mothers declined to a few dozen of the humbler and less informed wives and mothers whose luck it was to have husbands or sons still abroad or awaiting discharge. True, no longer were Casimiro and Pancho able to assess the club's hundreds of members a dollar in order to send an unfortunate gold star mother a five dollar bouquet of flowers. No longer were they able to collect fifty cents from each member in order to have a six dollar mass said for a fallen son or missing husband. But, with the membership falling off, by increasing the dues and assessments, the contributions and the quotas, and by giving dances to further the *veterano* cause, Casimiro kept meeting the payments on the many accounts he had opened for his many nieces and Pancho Pérez kept up the payments on his home.

One night Casimiro and Pancho sat in a little restaurant bewailing the proliferation of veteran's clubs when they overheard a veteran say "Damn, that Casimiro and Pancho must have really cleaned up while we were away. Some wives and mothers say that they even signed over allotment checks to them, to be kept in trust. Can you imagine?" "I sure wish I could see the Alliance of Mexican-American Christian Wives and Mothers' books," said another. "I'll bet. . . ."

Casimiro swallowed hard. To hear one's ancestry dishonored was one thing, but to speak of books and records . . . He lowered his head and said to his companion, "Alas, Pancho, they do not trust us. I think perhaps it would be best to disband the club."

"But we have gone too far for that," said Pancho. "I, for one, have many obligations. Anyway, haven't we been told that bingo soon be legalized? I'll bet we can. . . ."

"Didn't you hear?" asked Casimiro. "They spoke of the books. You were the one who kept them. . . ."

"WE," said Pancho. "WE. Don't you forget that. Both our signatures are on everything."

Casimiro slid down in his chair. "Keep your voice down," he said. "Whisper."

That very night, into the offices of the Alliance of Mexican-American Christian Wives and Mothers, two lone figures crept through opposite doors. Both quietly made their way to the desk where the box containing the books and the records of the contributions, dues, quotas, and assessments were kept.

Soon there was a scuffle, a knocking down of tables and chairs, a series of groans and grunts. A sleeping drunk was aroused and in the darkness ran into a parked patrol car, arousing a sleeping patrolman. By the time the drunk and patrolman arrived at the Alliance of Mexican-American Christian Wives and Mothers Club House and switched on the lights, Casimiro and Pancho were sitting opposite each other, panting like mountain climbers and too tired to move a muscle. Casimiro, scratched, uncombed, and disheveled, said, "W-w-we j-j-just f-fought a p-pair of th-theives m-m-mak-k-king off w-with our c-cash b-box and r-records."

"Y-y-yes. Th-thieves," added Pancho Pérez.

The following day the newspapers carried a full account of the affair as well as pictures. Casimiro, resembling a well fed convict, and Pancho, resembling an assassin, were written up as two heroes who had almost foiled a pair of robbers' plans. When the *Americanos* read the papers and saw the pictures, they said with slight smiles, "Mexican business."

Chicanos reading the papers muttered, *"Cabrones."* In their wrath some swore to . . . Others vowed to. . . .

In any case, for a long time nobody saw hide or hair of Casimiro Ancheta and Pancho Pérez. Rumor had it that they had skipped the country, that they were hiding, that they were dead. Alas, passions cool and. . . .

Months later, Casimiro sat in Pancho's office having his usual coffee and *pan dulce.* In a few hours his beloved Agripina would be home from work and this being her pay day, Casimiro had decided on supper at *La Golondrina Restaurant* and a Mexican movie. "Alas," sighed Casimiro, "Agripina is the love of my life." Pancho, in turn, was moaning the great number of queen candidates for the approaching Sixteenth of September. "To have so many queens robs the patriotic festivities of their significance," said Pancho. "I maintain that there should be but one queen."

In time the conversation turned to the subject of oppression and specially to a coyote named Carlos Vega who had cashed checks for wetbacks during the war, had reaped a fortune, and was now the business agent for the laborer's local. Carlos had naturally joined forces with another coyote named Julio Palafox, an ex-bootlegger who now had a very thriving *'migra* office uptown. Caught between these two coyotes a victim . . . Thus Carlos and Julio had become the darlings of incumbent as well as aspiring politicians. Lately they were engaged in forming the League of Mexican-American Clubs for Political Progress. "If they succeed in uniting the clubs, do you realize the killing they will make?" asked Casimiro. "God help our race from ever uniting under two such immoral, criminal scoundrels."

"Alas," sighed Pancho. "I don't get mad because they do it. It's just that . . . they don't invite."

AVELARDO VALDÉZ

TOMORROW IS HERE . . .

The dying fire fed from discarded six pack cartons and old lumber only partially illuminated and warmed the men who were huddled around its light, maintaining a vigilance they had held since early evening. On the periphery of this circle stood an individual obscured in the dark shadows of a cottonwood tree urinating against the caked summer earth.

"I remember when we were just kids, right before we entered the service," said Raúl who was bracing himself against the tree while delicately shaking his penis between his thumb and forefinger just before returning into the amber of the light. "It was different then; families were together and maintained a sense of dignity and respect."

Someone spit into the fire to reaffirm the statement and for an instant the flame roared and revealed their worn middle-aged faces, tailored, pegged trousers, plaid cotton shirts and pointed spit-shined shoes which were now either ruffled or covered with fine Texas dust from the driveway where they stood. The men mumbled in agreement as they passed around the last of the Mexican liquor whose bitter taste made them conscious of the approaching dawn and their weariness.

A few yards from the driveway was a one story woodframe house that most of the men identified as their home even after they had entered the service, married and begun to raise families of their own. Inside of this house, in the center where the families' activities were usually held, was a body pumped with chemicals, lying dead in a coffin. This body had represented to the five individuals a common identity and strength and now it was gone, creating a void that they had once visualized as a permanent reality.

The effects of a long night of excessive drinking and the strange seriousness of their voices made them scarcely audible outside of the immediate circle their bodies formed huddled around the small flames. But their conversation continued as it had throughout the evening—remembering their experiences as young boys shining shoes in downtown San Antonio, hustling young sailors and nickel hamburgers, and remembering long rides across town to play sandlot baseball that usually ended in a brawl; reminiscing of fights with rival barrios and family feuds that often resulted with tragic deaths, like an uncle they never knew who was stabbed to death in his early twenties, for a reason no one could ever explain. They spoke of Harlington on the outskirts of the city on Saturday afternoons where, if you could survive a round with white semi-pro boxers, you could make an easy five bucks. But, throughout the evening, their conversation was spaced by moments of silence when their thoughts went back to the man in the coffin. "It will no longer be the same when their generation is gone," said Ramón who traveled across several states with his entire family to attend the funeral.

The men present had families that were now half-grown and wives who were suffering from female complexities and all this made them realize that they were no longer young men and that the body lying in that house symbolized both a beginning and an end to some pre-determined destiny. They could not lean on the strength of that dead man and were coming to realize that they might have stopped doing so a long time ago (but never wanting to admit it to themselves) and that the man's last years were not spent in a child-like drunken senility in vain but because he was almost consciously preparing these men for this moment, a time when they would be forced to raise their own families so that their children would see them as they had once seen their elders.

It was a grave responsibility and, although they would be force to accept this fate, it was difficult to accept now, just hours before he was buried. Only after a full night of drinking and remembering old times would these men admit to themselves that this was why they were grieving, not for that body whose life would never return.

And as the dawn began to evolve, a cool breeze stirred the fire and sent a chill through the men that awakened them from their drowsiness. And they realized that one of the men was missing. He was the eldest son of the dead man and, as they began to look for him, the men heard a sobbing from inside the house. There they found Manuel cradling the dead man inside in his arms and kissing his face.

"Jesus Christ, Manuel, you'll awaken the women and children," someone said. But Manuel would not stop his weeping and the other men had to help pry him away from the body and coffin.

poetry

ABELARDO

AT 26000 FEET

días de lucha con sabor a chocolate
almas sin sangre—almas en pleno combate
machacando al racismo en un metate,
    ví llorar a mi hermano lágrimas rojas

danzando en aeropuertos por aztlán
ví desde el cielo en las nubes ese plan
oí a las montañas repetir su refrán,
    "él que nace pa' tamal, del cielo le caen las hojas"

en el horizonte busqué verdadera paz
el que se movía y yo me quedaba atrás.
buscaba un hombre que no trajera disfráz
    si andas en la lluvia, muy seguro que te mojas.

champaña, compadre y frijoles de olla
perros calientes y un caldito de cebolla,
jugo de ciruela pa'l gallo viejo que busca una polla.
    a ver que remedio dan pa' estas muelas tan flojas.

en la cáscara de un plátano escribí yo una poesía
entre más palabras le echaba menos era lo que decía,
pa' que entre dios al hombre falta que su alma este vacía.
    no es igual hechar mentiras que mentiras recojas.

GOING BACK TO EL BARRIO

having returned to good ol' el chuco, being back
for almost three weeks my yearning got the best of me
and yesterday eve i drove to la oregon, my favorite street,
paid my courtesies to el sagra church, talked with el niño dios
but found it hard to communicate with him as i had done before,
i went to la quinta corner and sat down for a spell
i wasn't there over five minutes when i recognized the wino smell.

préstame un daime (familiar phrase) the exact bus fare to hell . . .
paco crossed the street with a baby on each arm, proving all is well . . .
a game of touch (between traffic) was on, a player fell . . .
juan "mente" estrada comes along, he had not much to tell . . .
cheyene llegó y me saludó, iba al mono . . . barrio, such a beautiful cell
we never think of ourselves as prisoners . . . chavitos run, a distant bell
from the ice cream truck woke me up, i drove back to my hotel.

$

one dollar down
and one por los siglos de los siglos
way of life
of the so much per hour
and five dollars a baptism generation,
prices going up to heaven
instead of prayers.
insufficient funds,
gasoline and meat
     No no más no como yo
     sino que ni mi carro bebe.
dollar devaluation
god and gold and silver
       at an all time high
more taxes, less work
      tighter control
phase III of face I and II that didn't work
phase IV lurks
trigo to russia
    lumber to japan
       b-52's to cambodia
(i wonder if they fly on the same gas i don't have)
shower every other day
and water your lawn with beer
don't iron and watch tv at the same time,
cook on the sidewalk with el calor de sol,
sulphur and lead added freely to the free air,
the general electric demon joining el paso natural gas
which in turn joins humble oil
and all the demons of the dollar sign
preparing for a final feast
      with all of us
(ya ni podemos decir . . . dale gas . . .)
   no no más te sales, carnal . . . te vas.

TERESA PALOMA ACOSTA

FOR MAXIMINO PALOMO

the official history that
traces in pictures and words
endlessly depicts
in minute detail
the stealing of your honor
the selling of your manly labor
the pain you endured
as sons and daughters
drifted from you
met their death in the
hour of thorns and swords
will fail you

just as will history texts
written with the cutting pen of
palefaced brown/stone men who recall 1848
and
forget to tell about
men who cradled children to sleep
soothed their damp hair
told them stories
played la golondrina on his violin
and
laughed
aloud at dusk

UNTITLED

remember
that we have got to
shake our fists at life
whittle and sharpen the 2 X 4's of marina's legend
juana's history
make them forts that house our smiles

never refuse:
> to refuse
> the poets who scribble metaphors that possess
> to say that of late we have grown to loathe
> even the chiles verdes winking up from molcajete dungeons
> to say we shall raze the love factory
> and discontinue to create
> because we have got to

spend our time immersed
in the autumnal struggle of leaves that
fall/die/live again

remember that we have got to
push back the enchanted rock from sand castles
phrased in forever (more) vows
and turn away from the bullets
and turn away from the gray sheets
and pierce the dawn with ourselves

UNTITLED

i am watching night stars
landscaped permanently on television screens
the size that fit ali mcgraw eyes
jane fonda politics

night stars
that float lana turner-like across
media ads of clairol girls
vassar-voiced debutantes who fly in
from riviera holidays to walk
the socialist plank for an afternoon and
to party with the panthers.

i am watching night stars
playing roles in the traveling company shows
reaching back into pioneer days/yore days/folk ways
turned loose to say this is eden
turned loose to war with army boots and loaded rifles
on infantry folklore days
to say this is eden

i am watching doris (uh) day
lolling lightly on
rock hudson's bed whispering
"i am candy," rock
"a lollipop, a shirley temple dimple, a ribbon for you"

i am watching the polishers of floors in houses
without dirt
or
the hint of dust
named women who bark
"george, the insurance man is here
to take
his wedding dress
to markets for capital gains"
his tongue wags gross income
his eyes roll to the strains of
net profits

and i am thinking
will we turn out like these,

too?

es un dibujo de toda nuestra indiada
escrita en esa cara y
amplificada con pelo largo y rico
anunciando
recuerdos de aquellos ancianos abuelos
que se lo arrastraban por el suelo
una pluma azul
metidita por arriba (no más como antojito)

¡ay los tatoos que se ríen y lloran!
¡ay los anillos y pulsera que lo encierran!
¡ay ese paño de obrero y de rey!
como exclaman de las nubes de la pinta
lanzando gritos para todos los
encarcelados
sea en leavenworth
o austin
o seattle

y nos ha llegado
al pacito   al pacito
como lluvia dulce y primavera
platicándonos de lugares
donde se ha buscado
a veces encontrado
la flor creciendo
en el monte seco
o en las paredes
de casas martilladas con clavos derechosos
hirviendo con los ruidos gustosos
de todos esos muchachones de su niñez

es un dibujo de quince años
de ser el jardinero entre el fierro
allí enraizando las semillas
regándolas con plumas enojadas
haciendo brotar
sus matitas

y viéndolas enflorecer
se ríe al saber
que no hubo jarro bastante grueso
que pudo detener
su vino amoroso
con que él nos alimenta
con que él marca su tiempo
jalando/bailando/jalando
diciéndonos
ven acá
yo raúl soy

a veces el roy
un chicharrón de cuentos sabrositos (eso sí)
ven acá
te los doy

FOR SANTOS RODRÍGUEZ

¿cómo pasas tus días
mi cielo, mi cielo lindo?

pos jugando
corriendo
a donde crecen árboles de manzanas
a donde bailan las abejas
a donde se sientan los viejitos en el sol, fumand
a veces platico con el viento
con un gallo que me saluda por la mañana

¿y qué te han dicho todos aquéllos
mi cielo, mi cielo dulce?

pos que tiña retratos de ti y mamá sonriendo
que tenga sueños que enlacen el mundo con
el sarape color

¿y a dónde te me llevará la vida
mi cielo, mi cielo lindo?
¿a viajar como los vagos?
¿por mares de sangre?
¿por valles de pobreza?
¿ montañas del fuego negro?

¡pos no, papacito!
sino a donde el gallito cante sin temor
qui qui ri qui qui
a media noche

POEMA SOBRE RAÚL

es un dibujo de cuentos
pasados por la lumbre
cuentos de hombres
que han brincado
y saltado
sus canciones rojas y cafés
formando labores
de flores que cundieron
dentro'l fierro
de cuatro paredes silenciosas

sus pantalones bien cortados
bien usados
arrugados con vida
y sus botitas color de miel

caen con notas precisas
taleonando por los callejones
de viajes que nunca se acaban
diciéndose—no hay tiempo que perder

MY MOTHER PIECED QUILTS

they were just meant as covers
in winters
as weapons
against pounding january winds

but it was just that every morning I awoke to these
october ripened canvases
passed my hand across their cloth faces
and began to wonder how you pieced
all these together
these strips of gentle communion cotton and flannel nightgowns
wedding organdies
dime store velvets

how you shaped patterns square and oblong and round
positioned
balanced
then cemented them
with your thread
a steel needle
a thimble

how the thread darted in and out
galloping along the frayed edges, tucking them in
as you did us at night
oh how you stretched and turned and re-arranged
your michigan spring faded curtain pieces
my father's santa fe work shirt
the summer denims, the tweeds of fall

in the evening you sat at your canvas
—our cracked linoleum floor the drawing board
me lounging on your arm
and you staking out the plan:
whether to put the lilac purple of easter against the red plaid of winter-going-
into-spring
whether to mix a yellow with blue and white and paint the
corpus christi noon when my father held your hand
whether to shape a five-point star from the
somber black silk you wore to grandmother's funeral

you were the river current
carrying the roaring notes
forming them into pictures of a little boy reclining
a swallow flying
you were the caravan master at the reins
driving your threaded needle artillery across the mosaic cloth bridges
delivering yourself in separate testimonies.

oh mother you plunged me sobbing and laughing
into our past
into the river crossing at five
into the spinach fields
into the plainview cotton rows
into tuberculosis wards
into braids and muslin dresses
sewn hard and taut to withstand the thrashings of twenty-five years

stretched out they lay
armed/ready/shouting/celebrating

knotted with love
the quilts sing on

ALURISTA

SOMBRAS ANTIGUAS

shadows darkened by age
cast sueños antiguos
on wood fibers
on life nerves
path of corazón
independiente líquido sagrado
bajo el sol de rayos emplumados
la tierra de capas escamadas
los pechos, nourish mazorcas encueradas
maíz offerings
  to the temple of flesh
  to the temple of bones
mortal offerings
  to mortal bodies
  to corazones eternos
  to rostros mortales
peace exhaled by flowers in midafternoon
respeto a las carnes, huesos, y sangre
ajeno a la violencia ante el derecho
respeto a lo vivo y lo muerto
propio encuentro con reflejos apagados y oscuros
paz entre los vivos en la luz
eternal transformation
  never dead and gone: only absent flowersong

A OÍR RAZA

a oír raza
voy tus cantos
a ver raza
voy tus flores
en los campos
en los llanos
a oír y a ver
vamos raza
ríos raza ríos
  mares
calma encontramos
  entonces
en los mares corazones
calma encontramos
  entonces
en los sones y
en las flores

INDEPENDENCIA Y LIBERTAD

independencia y libertad
cadenas rotas
    la raza libre sobre
la tierra
    camina en busca
de nuestra nación
    oración al cielo
se eleva en cantos y lloros
    en las nubes se retuerce
y así el padre sol aparece
    la colonia ya perece
    y el barrio crece
se apresura el corazón
    a encontrar
    su sitio
nuestro sitio en el suelo
    the soil beneath
      us trembles
and freedom undercurrents
bathe
the earth's deepest caves
    all darkness in its
wetness
    seeks a light
      a sun to follow
a fence to break
    a pueblo to cultivate

LA VIDA O LA MUERTE

la vida o la muerte
    no existen
life hastens its pace
    onto death
death waits for the wheel
    to begin revolution
again
    in the carcass of
all matter
    the worms of life
are born
    to burn gusanos
into butterflies
    de colores brillantes
hijas del sol
    salen de la tierra
y en polvo
    convierten
    fértil polvo
dust turns with time
    and space remains
occupied
    flesh merely passes
      and huesos waited
        to pulverize
and be the wind
    to caress mariposas
      into papaloteadas
across the fleeting
    light of dusk

A PELEAR

a pelear
en la tierra
contra los pueblos
que conocen
lo mero principal
no he venido
a cultivar
lo mero principal
con los pueblos
he venido
regresado
a lo mero principal
de las cosas
y los seres
la energía
yóllotyl
corazón yoltéotl
corazón de luz ascendiente
luz que sube
que nace
que brota
en la base material
de las cosas
y los seres
el árbol de la vida
fruta energía
luz espiral
aliento cíclico
movedora raíz
lo mero principal
de las cosas
y los seres
y las naciones
y los pueblos
y los venados
y los pájaros
y las flores
y las abejas
y las hormigas
y las aguas
y las tierras
y los vientos
y los fuegos
y ! . . . lo mero principal

HACENDADO

hacendado
teamsters
safeway
imperio
violento
escuelas
televisión
instituciones
conciencia
violenta
tezcatlipoca yankee
yankee cuetes
cañones
bombas
aviones
yankee balas
ejércitos
policías
investigaciones
yankee sueños
pesadillas
gran ignorancia
amerikkka
amerikkka
amerikkka
kristianizante
kolonizante
kapitalizante
kondenado infierno
ya se retira
ya muere
parece el tezcatlipoca yankee

LA PAZ

la paz
tehachipi oasis
revolución morena
santas montañas
cantos lunares
llenos
corazones guerreros
guerrilleros chicanos
people
journey
long struggle
más
lo mero principal
gran conciencia
gran unión
amerindia
amerindia
amerindia
amerindia
santa tierra
tus guardianes
ya retornan
y ya nace
ya amanece el quinto sol

CAMINANDO VAN

caminando van
enfogonadas nubes
como elogio,
ha caído su sol
tras la montaña
río de valle
nevados murmullos
sonrisas derriten
vespertinas arrugas
cubren esta tierra
santa, papaloteando
hippies urbanos
herederos aún
del klan del penny
amerikkkano
buscan paz
nopales y arbustos
les desconocen
perros ládranles
sus padres sembraron
guerra, guerra
es, pues
que cosechan
mal de ojo

WHAT IT IS/IS WHAT IT DOES

what it is
ain't
what it was.
neither is it
what it will be.
what it is
is
what it does.
what it's done
is what it was
what it will be
is what it'll do.
what it'll do
will someday
be
when what does
is what it is.
del dicho
al hecho
mucho trecho
trecho hecho
hecho el dicho
dicho y hecho

MUJERES DE REBOZO

mujeres de rebozo colgantes niños
llorosos ojos . . . ciegos
cantos hambrientos
turistas tiendas
tenderos negocios . . . prósperos
boticarios talonean
sonrientes drogas
filereao's brazos
ambulantes corazones . . . perdidos
rostros opacos
todos corren
calles aceleradas
neones luces
todos corriendo
sin raíz
vereda
o fruto
fuera de la tortilla
diaria
lucha tostada
polvoriento sol
quema
pepsi-chorreados petates

NUBES DE LUCHA

si llamamos a las nubes
es pa'que nos traigan lluvia
es pa'que nos traigan lluvia
que llamamos a las nubes

le cantamos en la lluvia
le cantamos a la gloria
le cantamos a la gloria
le cantamos en la lluvia

y si vamo'a a ver la gloria
tenemos que hacer historia
tenemos que hacer historia
si vamos a ver la gloria

y si vamo'hacer historia
tenemos que hacer la lucha
hay que ponerle a la lucha
si vamos hacer historia

nuestra lucha aquí en la tierra
la mesmita que'n los cielos
la mesmita que'n los cielos
es la lucha aquí en la tierra

nuestra lucha es entre clases
es la mezcla de las razas
es la lucha entre culturas
de los hombres y mujeres

amerindia es la tierra
amerindios son los pueblos
amerindia es la lucha
amerindia es la causa

es la causa de las nubes
que riega amerindia lluvia
es la lucha de las flores
que brotan buscando gloria

LUNA LLENA

luna llena
crecientes
pueblos amerindios
amerindias tierras
tesoros palpitantes
escondidos
corazones estrangulados
vacas burguesas
máscaras pálidas
maquillaje de europeo
plasmadas, planteados
pintadas
plastados
corazones / rostros
    amerindios
    sueños
    tiran raíces en los suelos
    tienden ramas en los cielos
se levantan
se arman los pueblos
de conciencia
de sí
danzas con el propio corazón
luego con el de los otros seres danzas
danzas con madretierra corazón
con padre sol corazón danzas
relación/rama/raíz
    nación/ama/maíz
        maiztlán chilam balam
        maiztlán tonán el tollán
teotihuacán/tihuanaco/tepoztlán
danzas guerreras
contra ignorantes rostros
contra paralíticos corazones
amerikkkanas pesadillas
    disípanse
llueve lluvia luminosa
    dispérsanse oscuras
kolonias kapitalistas kristianizantes
amerindias naciones indígenas humanizantes
cultívanse
pa'dar fruto
    lucha amerindia
      amerindia causa
pa'nutrir raíces antiguas
árboles libertarios
únanse
  a
la lluvia

MANUEL CARO

YOU'VE COME HOME

You've gone home, Manuel,
And the corpsman couldn't understand
Your singing
"I've got sunshine on a cloudy day"
On Highway One,
Your arms in pain, your skin in shreds,
Your friend and the driver . . . dead.

You asked him a minute ago
If you could have some of the
c-rations on his truck.
And Willie,
Eighteen and Black,
Is cooked in the bed of the truck
While Gary from Kentucky,
Who hates "niggers,"
Rushes to your side and screams:
"If Willie dies, I'll kill every mother-
Fucking gook in this country!"

You've come home, Manuel,
You've come home.

TO WILLIE

I didn't mean to bore you
With all the things I've said.
I needed someone to understand
The reasons why I'm dead.

I didn't mean to waste your time;
I wanted you to know.
How slow . . . and miserably painful,
The grass above me grows.

I didn't mean . . . believe me,
I didn't mean for you to cry.
The pain becomes more bearable
Once we've died.

OH MIGHTY SOLDIER WHERE DID YOU STRAY?

Oh, mighty soldier, where do you stray?
Glory and honor are the other way.
Stand the blood, the stench of dead,
The crumbled bodies and rolling heads,
The children's tears, whose cries we hear
Above your prayers and silent fears.
And, ere I ask, yet unknowing,
Oh, mighty soldier, where are you going?

TO ELENA

Elena,

Who pumps gas and people's minds,
she lives around the block.

Elena, who asks but never asks,
who understands and doesn't,

Elena . . . ?
She lives around the block.

UNTITLED

I wanted to write a happy poem,
Hint at clichés about warm summer breezes
and love.
And soft guitars, rancheras,
And long walks in public parks
With white girls
More Mexican than me.

I wanted to write a happy poem,
Hint at clichés about warm summer breezes,
and love.
A happy poem
About me.

WHERE YOU THERE MY LORD, WHEN THEY CRUCIFIED US?

In Jesus Christ our Lord.
Amen.
The mass would end;
God became a man again.

We'd leave the mass.
And God was there.
God . . . I was told . . .
Was everywhere

Time passing . . .
Still believing, childhood dreaming.
Praying that the war would end.
Hoping he would end the screaming
Sounds of all those men.

Time passing . . .
Disbelieving, childhood dreaming.
Tattered threads and fields of red
Adorn the souls of shattered men

Time passing . . .
Fear revealing . . . god deceiving
All those countless men.
In their screaming, praying
To a repugnant air.

UNTITLED

If god had been a faggot,
Where would you be?
If god had been "that nigger,"
That "spic" around the block,
That chink across the hallway,
Or an easy fuck,
Where would you be?
That whore across the street,
Who, if we didn't use her,
Would climb between the sheets
without you . . . without me,
Where would she be,
If god had been a whore?

TO "FATHER CASEY"

En el nombre del padre.
Chinga tu madre.
Espíritu santo.
    Amen.

MY DAD

We never got invited for dinner at Mr. Dolan's
My Dad's boss.
We cleaned his yard or basement.
Hauled out the trash.
I always heard my father say
how kind he was
Threw away "good" stuff
along with all the other junk
We'd put in our garage,
    If mom didn't see anything she wanted.

Other white people
whose yards we cleaned,
Always seemed to ask, If we knew so and so.
Another "Spanish Fellow."
And Dad would look away
And put his hands into the tops
of his trousers.
Pulling them up he'd say,
No . . . no can't say that I do.
And he'd feel bad because he didn't
And because he thought white people
talked to each other that way.

We were always rushing to the dump;
Just before it closed
Because Dad worked until five,
Or Oscar, my brother needed shoes,
Or Mom needed five more dollars
for food stamps.

When we'd go shopping
Dad never went in . . .
He always made some excuse.
So I would stand in line
And suffer the humility
When Mom would say to the cashier,
"I have food stamps."

Dad lived alone, when we went to the orphanage,
Because Mom went to the State Hospital.
"To become a better mother"
or so she told us.
And probably because she got so tired
Waiting outside the cantinas
all those Fridays,
while we went in
to get my dad

REFLECCIONES HACIA MI BARRIO

Poema dedicado a toda Raza
cual se encontró, halló, se miró,
buscó, se vendió, se resaltó,
etcétera . . . .
hasta el punto de que se perdió
en esta época.

Guitarras, lloren, Guitarras . . . .
As Poetic Barrioations
Rhythmically reverberate
from within the echoes
of your soul.

Where your past, present, and future,
Cataclysmically collide into being;
Where one becomes ones' self
in the Barrio of ones' soul,
Reevaluating remembrances of things
that were, are, and should have been!
(Ese bato, allá te wacho en la esquina)

La Esquina,
Educational implementator
for survival . . . .
Where young Chicanos
                han,
                        están,
y seguirán jugándola fría;
learning the facts of life,
Where the educational environment is
and is not too a la americana,
and still through
sufferings, hungers, and strife;
manage to survive . . . . jugándola fría bato.
(si no la juegas fría bato, te vamos a quebrar.
arroz corazón, te bañaste o así hueles siempre.
los ruquitos estarán locos, pero saben en donde están!)

Our Viejitos,
Cultural roots of our existence,
with so much to offer,
                so much to say,
to closed ears within enclosed minds

in worlds of their own . . . .
y que mañana se acaba el mundo,
and who is to say,
for is it not they
that have endured?
(Pos si yo era Dorado de Villa.
Y yo Zapatista.
Eso era vivir.)

Y los Jefitos
desmadrándose por el pan nuestro
de cada día,
to the beat of no ser y es ser,
(Por qué yo Dios mío, por qué yo.
si Dios quiere, algo más nos dará.
llegará el día, ya verás el día llegará.)

And such is our existence
day to day living,
day to day being,
day to day struggling,
For yet another day to day . . . .

And then;
          from deep within the chasms
of el Barrio
an infant cry was heard;
                    (Déjame ser.)
a questioning voice rising;
                    (¿Y yo qué?)
a people bellowing;
                    (Raza, Raza, Raza!)
a mestizo nation awakening;
                    (¡Ya me cansé!)
to the ill-guided misrevelations,
of sociological misinterpretations,
And still,
          while others struggled on,
some of us were tokenistically toriquiados
into governmental manipulation . . . .
And of this we cried out,
while others sold out,
and still others were bought out,
(Y por qué no bato,
                es parte de la cultura,
                              se vale ese.)
Y we were torn,
               tattered,
                      and lost,
     from movimiento,
               to movidamiento,
                         from movidamiento,
     to movimiento,
               from movimiento,
                         to movidamiento,

carnal quemando, rechazando, y chingando a carnal;
under auspices of relevancy and legitimacy
to the tune of H.E.W., O.E.O., and etcétera! ! ! ! ! !
(Y se vale bato,
                    nomás es por un ratito,
¿acabo qué es una quemada?)
Damn but it hurts
to be hurt from inside! ! ! ! ! !

And I learned
              to love,
     to hate,
to hate,
     to love,
LOVE/HATE . . . .
until both became
one and the same,
              and who is to blame,
who is to blame . . . .
Suddenly to all that was
and all that seemed to be
an indigenous nation endogenously
Proclaimed;
           I can not,
               I will not,
                  I shall not,
be as you say!
           For I already am,
                 I AM;
                        YO SOY! ! ! ! ! ! !
Mestizo,
        Hispano,
               México-Americano,
                     Pocho,
               Pachuco,
          Indio,
     Chicano,
I am a Cosmic entity
                 of all combined,
and yet not one of a kind . . . .
I am a revelation to man!
from my Kingly Aztec past
to my Chicano presencia;
I am here,
           not only to be,
but to last,
           and I shall last! ! ! ! ! !
AY,
    AY,
        AY,
            AY,
               AY! ! ! ! ! ! !
Y Arriba Raza . . . .
                    Huelga Campesino . . . .

Vámonos recio . . . .
                    Todo o Nada . . . .
Sí Se Puede . . . .
                    Tierra y Libertad . . . .
Boycott . . . .
                    Abajo con sistemas opresivos . . . .
Y de marcha en marcha;
                    demonstration to demonstration,
we had come into our own . . . .

Y El Movimiento lingers on,
and is alive and well
en el corazón . . . .
While El Chuco is torn and scattered,
Mientras Raza hopes are shattered,
While Companies explode Families,
(que gacho de los presidios que explotaron)
Mientras Dallas destroys Chicano minds;
(Oíste del niño Santos)
and who knows what other desmadre
against us we can find . . . .

Sí, El Movimiento still lingers on,
and is very much alive,
                    and we shall survive,
                              carnales,
we shall survive . . . .
                    Ultimately . . . .
all that is left to be
is our humanity . . . .

Now, allow Poetic Barrioations
to Rhythmically Reverberate
from within the echoes
of your soul! ! ! ! ! ! !

Sí, Guitarras, lloren, Guitarras . . . .
                    Por qué no . . . .

VERONICA CUNNINGHAM

when all the yous
of my poetry
were really
she or her
and
i could never
no
i would never
write them
because
of some fears
i never even wanted
to see.
how could i have been
that frightened
of sharing
the being
     and
       me.

poor animal
small cage
and
a smaller
knowledge
yet
of love.
that combination
gives
you
a pet —
to care for
when you've a need
that combination
gives
you
a security
at the expense
of your pet
and
his freedom
that combination
scares
the hell
out
of me
and
i find myself
not trusting
anyone's
kindness
or touch.
for i fear
poor animals
and
small cages
and
almost love . . .

. . . almost love . . .

i am losing
my laugh
i have already
lost
my patience
and
i am violently
silent
against
you.

love all you can
hurt will soon
make
the time
for you
to try
        and
                understand
love
and at least
hurt
for a reason

someday
when
i finally find you
leaning
in a corner
and
alone
i'm gonna smile
a smile
that will bring
you home.

you become such
a different
bottle
when
you drink
a little wine
you always
end
the night
by smashing
yourself
against
what you think
you should be
and
i just remember
broken bits
of glass
where we once
innocenced
to pass

six hours later
and
the night
has my day
yawning
between grins
six hours later
where
are you now?
if you've gone
to bed
to catch
something
we couldn't
well,
go ahead
    and
    sleep
we knew
we wouldn't.

always
is
for some
a way
of life
for others
always
is
a way
to avoid
  and
    live.

          all the winds
          could whisper
          peace
          and
          all the winds
          could shout
          of it
          but
          deaf mankind
          won't
          hear
          of kind mankind
              and
               peace . . .

heaven isn't very far
away
it's as close
as hell

who do i look
at them
to chart
my dreams?
they always
speak
with grim
    grey
words
of shattered securities
so bitter
so hurt
so discouraged
so pained
so fragile
so skeptical
but
so human.
my dreams
always
become like
fugitives
away
from the real world
and away
from them
for awhile . . .

the people around me

are we all so fragile
that we love
for alliance
and
not for love's sake
but
for the deepening
of the valley
and
of the rut

                                        how can your eyes
                                        say
                                        what i hear?
                                        you really
                                        are
                                        so far
                                        away,
                                        why is it
                                        i feel
                                        you so near. . . .

. . . love

LLEVAN FLORES

Llevan flores en los dientes
    tigres y arañas frías.

Muy poca gente llora
            (la esquina pide silencio)
        y los perros ladran tristes
        en el barrio de los pobres.

Esquinas de puños huecos
        ¡ladran Chicano Power!

En la tumba solitaria
        las flores no se marchitan.
        El joven de bronce un día
        No muerde mosaicos fríos.

Mientras batos y poetas
        llenan de dulces frescos
        (¡Ay! ¡Son de cariño y odio!)
        una piñata vieja —
                un bato en las esquinas
                halla plomo en sus heridas.

llevan flores en los dientes
        tigres y arañas frías.

PULGA
(who wears a blue moon on her knee)

Pulga Pulgita Pulg
The soul of the river sings

The heads of the wheat they gleam
As dragonflies made of gold

The river the river called
And down the road i came
        (brushes and paint in a paper sack)

Pulgita i dreamed
        by the river i dreamed Pulgit

Pulga Pulgita Pulg
The soul of the river sings

61

NO NO NO

the wind.
it is no longer quiet.
it is no longer still.
it pounces. it raids. it rams.
with deafening clamor it seems to bellow
          NO

          NO

               NO
how brutal its slam! how tapered its sorrow!

it scourges itself,
desperately clawing its inward Self
into a stinging morass of fury.

it charges! out of the night
                    as glossy black toros dart
searching the banderillas.

it crushes itself against the face
of slightly unmovable bricks . . .
of stones, of hearts, of flowers.
it writhes in dark cOnVuLsIoNs.
how SHOCKING its grating. how blunt.

it madly lunges against my window —
     and SPLATS! against it
          moaning
out of its mirror glaze
     no . . . no . . . no . . .

Unwillingly i peer deep . . . !
     NO

          NO

               NO

. . . unfamiliar eyes . . . dark and intense
stare back . . .

the thing at the window moans
     No   No   No

LAS HUELLAS DE MIS PASOS

¿Has visto las huellas que dejan
los seres en el tiempo?
Sabes, yo creo haberlas visto una vez.
¿Recuerdas aquella noche que hablábamos
sobre tu vida y la mía?
Esa noche, embriagado por el sagrado éxtasis de tus besos,
traté de desandar mi propio destino
y caminé, caminé, caminé . . .

El Cielo, ¡ah, el Cielo!
Parecía ser el Principio.
Y Yo, Yo creí ser Él.
Esa noche fui cielo, nube, tormenta,
tierra, pez, planta, fuego, hombre, Dios.
Todo fue como un vértigo,
perdí la noción del tiempo, de las cosas.
No había secretos, sólo existía La Verdad.

Esa noche, Mujer, escuché el eco de mis pasos.
Mas al querer ver mis huellas
me dí cuenta que un pequeño oleaje de agua las iba borrando.
Insistí en volver a verlas por un tiempo indefinido, y . . .
mi cuerpo . . . se estremeció de miedo.
El pequeño oleaje se había convertido
en un inmenso Río.
Pensé en Ti y apresuré el paso.
De pronto,
mis ojos se encontraron estrellados
y me sentí flotar en inmenso océano terrenal.

Esa noche, el fulgor acarició dos almas,
y por fin pude ver las huellas de mis pasos.

MI COMPAÑERA Y YO

Anoche cuando !eía
mi Compañera me habló en silencio.
Su suave, amorosa y lúgubre voz,
insistía en ausentarme de la lectura.

No quería hacerle caso y prendí
la lámpara que tenía a los pies
de mi humilde y acogedor lecho.
Pasó un largo silencio y de pronto
sentí nuevamente su presencia.

Extendí la mano derecha para asegurarme
de que estaba prendida la lámpara
que está a la cabecera de la cama
y sentí que alguien me la cogía
y me la besaba suavemente.
Aparté la vista del libro y
miré amargamente a la pobre intrusa
que se mostraba ante mí
ruborizada y ansiosa de amor.

La miré cara a cara.
Ella palideció al verme y noté
que se había avergonzado.
Me le acerqué suavemente para no espantarla,
la cogí del brazo y le ofrecí asiento al borde
de mi cama. Ella, con la vista baja,
se dejó conducir y se sentó apaciblemente.

Le expliqué sobre lo que leía
y al ver el regocijo con que sus ausentes ojos
me envolvían, sentí un calor friolento
que agitó mis venas y me estremeció el alma.
Salí de mi turbación y sin insinuarle que sentía
simpatía hacia ella, por temor a que se enamorase de mí,
le pedí que explicara el motivo de su visita
y del por qué rehuía mi mirada . . .

Ella, con trémula y quebrantada voz y sin
alzar la vista, me explicó que llevaba 27 años
observándome y que me quería con toda su
inexistente alma. Cariñosamente la cogí
de la mejilla y le alcé suavemente
el covernoso rostro sonrosado.

Pensé por un momento haberla escuchado sollozar
pero había sido el breve y dilatado zumbido
de una palabra sufrida que se perdía en la infinidad del libro.

—No temas — le dije calladamente al oído.
—Nunca debes de rehuir mi vista ni mis pasos.
Leo acerca de ti, proque pienso en ti.

Quiero saber todo lo que a ti se refiere,
quiero llegar a ti sin temor ni dudas,
quiero sentirme digno de ti.
Quiero que cuando tú y yo crucemos
el espacio, así como esa palabra
que se ha perdido en la eternidad,
lo hagamos por un tiempo indefinido.

Así como tú has estado conmigo
desde mi principio,
así quiero que continúes hasta mi fin.
Quiero que estés en mí como yo en ti,
comprendiéndonos y amándonos
hasta que los dos nos volvamos uno
. . . Nada.

La cogí en los brazos,
me la acerqué al pecho,
sentí que me desprendía el alma.
Cuidadosamente la extendí
en las páginas de mi lecho,
y ahí, los dos nos confiamos
al ritmo eterno del universo.

MI HIJO

—Mi niño, ¿adónde va?
—To school.
—To school, y por qué vas tan triste?
—Because.
—Because, ¿por qué?
—Because I don't like school.
— ¡Qué no te gusta!
Pero, ¿por qué no te gusta?
—Because the teacher hates me
and don't like the school, it
is ugly.
—Wait, wait, un momentito.
A ver, a ti no te gusta la escuela
porque está fea y el maestro, dime
¿por qué es que el maestro no te quiere?
—I don't know why. But he is always
hitting me with a ruler; he pulls my
hair, my ears; he sends me to the principal;
he says that I am no good, that I should
stay at home instead.
—¿Cómo se llama ese viejo que te ha dicho todo
eso?
—Is not a viejo, is a vieja, and,
I can't remember the name.
Es un nombre que se oye muy feo.
—¿Cuántos años tiene usted mi hijito?
—Seven.
—You know something, yo quisiera decirte
munchas cosas, pero, pero no creo que las
puedas entender muy bien. Pero, mira,
¿ves ese banco nuevo y esos edificios
recién construídos a media cuadra de tu escuela?
—Yeah.
—Bueno ahora mira tu escuelita,
¡qué viejita y chiquitita que está!
¿Verdad?
—Ajá.
—Mira, ni siquiera tiene columpios,
ni un pedacito de zacate o tierra donde juegues.
¡Ah!, ahora mira hacia esa universidad que está allá
pasando el semáforo que está en rojo
¿Ves todo ese zacate verde que está alrededor y por entre
la universidad? Sépalo hijo, ahí nadie juega,
sólo está de adorno or sirve de vez en cuando
para que se echen y reposen tus futuros maestros,
y los hijos de bancos y futuros edificios.
En esa universidad hay pisos alfombrados y
asientos forrados. Las aulas son grandes
y se chismea por ahí, que los maestritos
son los mejores del mundo.

—¿Why don't I have a school like that?
Why do people build new banks and other
buildings and not a new school for us?
Why don't I get a new chair?
Why can't I have swings and grass
to play on?
—Yes mi hijo, I see that you have
a lots of preguntas. I know
the answers to some of them. But,
pero yo que puedo hacer. Somos
pobres y aquí parece ser que no
se nos quiere. Someday, when you
grow up y seas todo un hombre,
comprenderás.
Come on, lift up your face y
nunca bajes la vista ante nadie.
  Sí, papá.
  Ande hijo, siga adelante,
y que Dios lo bendiga.
—Adiós, mi niño.
      Cuidado, ahora sí, anda, ya
      no hay tráfico, el semáforo
      está en verde y nada te pasará.

DOMINGO BRIGHT MORNING

Tú, hueles a makeup en la cara
y el aire se acerca a tus mejillas
callado.
Yo, camino guachando cabeza baja
a tu lado.
A la iglesia Romana —
en esquina del callejón
que desecramos los batos
anoche sin tiempo.
Palmas guardianas cerca de
la torre mocha están —
barrio Chicano,
Dios judío,
Virgen india
iglesia Chicana.

"Ellos no necesitan la amistad
porque no la conocen"
Quisiera yo pasar por la iglesia;
la religión me jala.
Por la Iglesia no se pasa,
se es;
mi pensamiento entra
la cola de mi ángel de la guarda
me atrasa.

Suenan tus ropas de raso,
sudan los dedos al libre
de rezos,
cuentan el tiempo tus pasos al paso.
Guadalupe me espera;
sus ojos negros sobre ti,
Guadalupe, Lupe, Lupe, Lupe, Lupe.
Virgen de la Macarena con música mexicana;
tú; cuenta sus pasos esta mañana.
Lupe, Lupe, Lupe,
ángeles prietos siempre supe,
que me quieres la quieres,
nos quieres
Virgen de flores virgen de amores.
Puertas de dos —
goznes de fierro
arriba:
Por esta puerta pasan los mejores cristianos,
they happen to be Chicanos:

Lasciate ogni speranza, voi chéntrate!
si no te detienes,
Última chanza
no cierres la puerta antes de que
termine de entrar,
me agarras la cola . . .
adentro se reirá la bola.

Ella se adelanta, el pueblo canta.

"O María, madre mía
o consuelo del mortal"

María ojos, azules se alegra;
le cantan las mañanitas
Lupe no se encela.
El pueblo, los batos, las chavalas
a la güera cantan . . .
pero en los corazones Chicanos
la Santísima Virgen de Guadalupe
manda.

Per ómnia sáecula saeculórum —
¡Ay! tarde llegué
Blanco y negro, negro y blanco
la Raza hincada cruza los brazos;
la sala apretada de mi gente.
Raza con rezos rezando.
Ruca, la ruca ha llegado conmigo;
missa solemnis.
Cabello negro gente prieta,
manos suaves velas de cera; aroma,
flores con los ojos bajos quietos.

She,
She speaks English,
she raps English,
she reads English,
she sits English,
pero quiere en español.
Sueña en español,
piensa en español,
va a la church en español,
juega en español,
works in English,
siente en español,
drive in English,
hace cariños en español,
runs in English . . . .
se mece en las curvas de sus pasos en español.
Mira, Ay! ¡Mira! en español.
Duerme, duerme chula
únicamente en español.

RUCA FIRME LIBERATED

"No me digas," me decía,
"que no te hable de mis sueños,
de lo que quiero ser,
de no tener dueños."
De Chamaca nunca me puse calzones,
me subía en los árboles
jugaba beisbol con los batos
nunca me puse vestido, sólo pantalones.

Quiero ser libre Amor,
libre, ser un ser,
sola pero nunca sin ti.
Quiero sentir lo que siento,
buscar y hacer lo que quiero
amar tal como siento,
tener mi propio pensamiento.

Sola sí, pero dentro de mí.
Contigo también, nunca sin ti.
dos en uno mi viejo,
pero entiende, siempre hacer
nada más, sencillamente lo que quiero.

A UNA CHAVALA CHICANA COMO PERLA

Quiero estar solo en medio del desierto,
donde la vida está y se mueva en silencio.
Quiero para escoger un lugar donde no haya nadie más,
que sea mi templo donde vengo con cariño noble
a presenciar un amor tierno,
sin witness más que yo
y la naturaleza callada,
Para decir únicamente

*Te Quiero Preciosa
Chavala Chicana.*

Estás lejos.
El Tiempo, nuestro padre a quien obedecemos,
distancia que mide nuestros sentimientos
ha reducido mis emociones a ti a lo más básico, primordial:
tanto que me es realidad natural y fácil
depositar ante lo más puro que puedo encontrar
en la naturaleza creada y creadora
lo que más aprecio sin tiempo: mis amores.

Quiero que todo sea en silencio.

Esto lo sabrás también sin palabras
cuando con mis acciones y mis ojos, ahora buenos,
te digan lo que con tiempo ahora sin medida siento.

Hemos pasado más alla de aquellas veces
en que tú y yo hacíamos grandes cosas
en grandes y estallados instantes.

Ha madurado nuestro amor:
ahora lo mece el tiempo;
por eso ya no tiene más
principio ni fin: ahora sencillamente *es.*

Felíz eres; analógica y clara y risueña
como la vida plena y bien fulfilled.
Mejor te amo en silencio − y dejemos
con unspoken words *querernos.*

CHAVALA CHICANA QUE SE ALEJÓ SIN EXPLICACIÓN

Amor Mío:
You have chosen to be silent sin tiempo, sin límite,
mas yo mido con los movimientos del corazón, no el tiempo
sino las cosas que pudieron ser, y con ese tiempo movimiento
espero igual.
¿ves? Encarcelado en los límites de la esperanza
y sin rienda mis deseos
de que mis ojos se llenen de ti.
Gozo para siempre habrá cuando ante mí en un instante
sin measure te vea y estés.
En ese *sólo* serás eterna,
y yo su witness extasiado.
En ese *único* serás virginal
y yo creador universal.
En ese *cuando* serás madura fruta
y yo la tierra que te recibe.
En ese *allá* serás el cielo cuya
cortina lejana sin medida
llegue a su baja mitad
donde estoy yo.
Más me mueve el amor que múltiple alcanza
forma indecisa y perfecta
con pensar en ti, formarte en mi mente
y lo que me hace temblar
por ti: Eso pesa,
         Eso cuenta,
         Eso vale.
Más vivo en lo que me hace
tremendo, es decir: vivo y extático.

UNTITLED

Tú, guardas silencio en la esfera
al fin de la distancia
de donde te veo a donde estás
no pain, no worry, no want —
sólo las burbujas de mi mente proceso
que te ven no pudiendo con los ojos.
porque además de ti siendo.
Porque agregado a tu ser.
Pues considerando tu existencia.
Ya que inevitable permaneces bella.
Además de lo que conozco de ti, una perla.
Porque eres armonía entre lo infinito
y de lo que la tierra nace creación.
Porque al pensar en ti causas tonos
y de forma alguna siempre canción.
Porque eres una inmensidad Cosita,
y porque no sé que más . . .
Paso más allá del te amo . . . te quiero,
mira pues, por eso.

UNTITLED

Las chavalas, parece, siempre quieren ir al mar
y este las llama incesante.
Tú, te meces en las olas del mar
que yo recuerdo.
Tú, creo que naciste a la orilla.
Tú, invocas, aunque no lo sabes,
en silencio, el movimiento curvo de las olas;
ola que a la nada arrullan.
Por ahí, en esa nada, naciste —
     la cuna fue la espuma
que interminable cambia;
siempre nueva,
en abstracciones el mar, con eso,
viste a la chavala chicana
con ropa cambiable que siempre lleva.
Tú naciste en el mar — tú naciste a la mar.
Tú naciste al mar — al mar — tú naciste al mar al mar.

UNTITLED

El cacto silencioso roca raíces
en la loma que ostenta marisma cercamar
me guacha cuando voy a verte
perla de piel sudor sol dorado high noon.
Silencio sin boca alto ángulos verdes
espinas cortamiento
habla sin programa brisa voluntaria.
Quisiera vivir contigo chavala del mar,
no sueño sino aliento fuerte en pautas
de música sangre lo dicen.
Perfil de quehaceres la casa está bien
también perched esperando elementos
de la vida tu humedad
mi tierra siembre labrada.

BATO Y CHAVALA CHICANA AL MAR

Solamente una vez al mar fuimos tú y yo,
acababa de llegar yo de la distancia
a donde tú vivías paciente,
hermosa, en la loma del pueblo.

Junto al mar
con los pies sobre la arena
mirando el mar lejano ondulado
con los dedos finos contando del suelo los granos.

Silenciosos estábamos, poco a poco
nuestro amor meaning saliendo,

nuestros corazones latidos esperando
se acoplarán en uno-seres queridos.

Chavala chicana gota de perla:
más silencio ha pasado entre los latidos
de nuestros corazónes
que palabras perdidas dichas sin sentido.

Nomás esto quería decirte, Esa,
pa recordarte donde estoy
no digas nada hoy;
let me be —
que te diga hoy lo que fuimos by the sea
y que de ahí salgan otras cosas.

UNTITLED

Chavala Chicana que va a tener un hijo con bato
y no saben que hacer pero están locos.

Llevas m'ijo.
No sé que va a pasar. Llevas m'ijo dentro.
Más bien tú y nuestro hijo son dos, van juntos. Están juntos.
Son juntos.
Ha sucedido, que en tu cuerpo se ha realizado la naturaleza;
eres la naturaleza y nuestro hijo es el fruto único.
Vive dentro de ti, pequeñito y silencioso.
En unos cuantos días te has hecho más hermosa que nunca.
Eres hermosa ahora por fuera porque siempre
fuiste una perla, como una perla,
por dentro porque tu bondad siempre
te llenó. Eres naturalmente buena.
Más hermosa aun porque llevas en ti la creación,
una nota musical silenciosa de la vida.
Esperas. Espero. Mas, mientras esperamos hay una música
enorme y suave que nos mece con felicidad.
Hay un vaivén de gusto en nuestros ojos porque tenemos
mejor razón de ser felices: tenemos un hijo.
Un hijo que no ha nacido aún.
Un hijo que hemos los dos depositado en ti, no sólo en tu
cuerpo, sino también en tu todo, más aún; en tu alma.
Ahí estará por algún tiempo madurándose hasta que tú des
fruto al mundo este, de fuera.
Has hecho el eterno rito de germinar semilla para que
exista la vida.
Con Dios te has squared y estás bien.

CONSEJO DE BATO A BATO

Bato: cuida a la chavala que te quiere.
A guy no sabe cuando puede cambiar el viento
y lo que hoy bien se tiene
se desamarra y a menudo se pierde.
Cuando contigo ella es tender,
recuerda bato y aprende.
Deja que sus cariños dentro de ti,
          despacio   vayan
y si tú la quieres, eso que entra
será alimento de su fruta;
cuando estés solo te sentirás firme.
Un bato puede vacilar cuando
                    vacilan,
mas cuando hay cariño
un buen hombre, bato firme,
no juega con las mujeres.

"Chavala chicana original altar
bato con ella hace pareja caminar"

Sale el sol y dios por la mañana,
shadows long over the rough.
Estoy completo con mi thought.
Duermes hoy día de amor
Wedding song awaits los dos
Seda y mums diciembre llama
sun on frost it melts on on
it's agua.

Soy yo con canto, mirando al sur verde
inmensidad amazona alimentada de ríos
capacidad azul de cielo above
cayendo slow
verde, azul a punto de un color
alguien, algo, nada con
redondas suena violón
Nace la medida de veinticuatro
horas para un tú y yo esperando
de estatual priest con buena mano
sobre nuestras cabezas suave bendición.
Epitalamio del sagrado azul cosmos
con germinal calor
abajo verde land en un amor.

Dedo de above tocando
la tierra madre a punto de germinando
hoy tiempo
hoy tú y yo
catedral redonda todo el mundo.
quieto callando,
quieto sin movimiento esperando
tú un sí
yo, al instante lo mismo que oí.
Ayer no lineal más redondo
solo, estando de pie medio del desierto
hoy igual y curvo nada ha muerto.
You await y esperas duality brown
skin al aire dando
buenos días saludando
descalza pelo largo cayendo
por la superficie de dios
a pasos contados en sueños
                    caminando
Yo alentado con el aire de dios,
cuate de carne y amor
escondido en el arrullo del sueño orfeón
Canto
cada paso que das
al centro del templo esperando.
Desierto adiós
Germen de dos un color acercando.
De flores sensación

olor flotando
radial con los dos al centroyendo.
instante raro momento estraño
anillo de amor cierra nuestro año
átomo solo
celebremos la vida
con colores
aire en todas partes, ida y venida
fragancias aloft
aguas onduladas among us
Priest de cera on top con vela
y candela
cábula sagrada en silencio
Batos con ojos de sapo
chavalas con ojos de ranas
Empieza hoy lo nuevo, vida rara
vuelvo al día del empezar.

Tú hueles a make-up en la cara
yo camino contigo cabeza abajo
dominado por tu bondad chavala.

JUAN GÓMEZ-QUIÑONES

OCTUBRE 1967, A CHE

los arrieros
    se ven
cruzando el monte
    son llagas en el sol,
ayer pasó
    la sangre por la tierra,
Perú-Bolivia
    donde se contaba
    con nudos
    el tiempo, el dinero y el espacio.

My father's land
        is crossed
ribbon like
by stone fences
        that wither in the sun.
White stones that glisten in the sun,
Stones that ballast a sea of brown
    hills.

My father's whip laid them,
My mother's tribe fed them.

CANCIÓN

Las mariposas
No cantan, dibujan luz
Otoño viene.

OCTUBRE

Leaves burnt, smoke
Autumn days that recall you
time, why is it?

DÍA OBRERO

El sol enfermo
silbido color ceniza
Hombres a casa.

78

Las viejas milpas
deshojan campesinos,
Son vientos nuevos

MÉXICO, 1971

los perros ladran.
sus voces corren por las escaleras
de este México frío y solitario.
Este año siento la humedad más
       que nunca.
Una voz tosca que se estrella contra
       las paredes: calla.
Los perros ladran,
sus reclamas son piedras contra
       la luna.

BARRIO SUNDAY

No violence then
When afternoon led to afternoon
our frontiers were marked
House to corner
corner, two, three blocks
then home again.

No violence then
When sundays pirated to another world
each faced the others
smiles flickering like blades
on gaping streets that
       glistened like glass.

No violence then
When in the arrogance of innocence
       each felled the other.
       Not child's fortune I,
I survived one afternoon to see my
       prison in the morning glare
That is why
there is violence now.

FROM AUSTIN TO HOUSTON

In the bright pain of a
      Texas sunset,
I felt the humid weight,
      Moss on trees.

How tedious after one hundred and
      thirty-seven years
Each day like a stone.
Lonely houses of flaking paint,
      littered alleys.

Austin you must have savored
      pride, then.
The unseeming Mexican has
      worn you thin and reedy.

Mocking laughter drips through
      the night
Desperate women-girls gamely play,
      the role of the role of their mothers,
         who learned it through admonishment.
The men draw in, exchange spent anger.
Boisterous, hollow as casings
They have a furtive glance, life
      is a smoker.
The best take an advanced degree
      in divinity.

Texas is a land of lonely houses
      scattered with people
Huddled along roads.

I love to see the secret
      white houses of Austin.
Snail shells set-off by river stones.

Sobre tierra rica
Colorada cae la lluvia violenta

TO D

That afternoon
 along the shore
 while the ocean
 fed from your hands
I knew then
 its color could never be
 as many hued as your eyes
nor
 its roar be
 as ominous as your smile.

•

TO R

Ese otoño — eras
  como cuando te
  conocí
  llena de tristeza.
Como el vuelo de la gaviota,
  como espiga que se
  cae,
  como ruido lejano en
  la noche.

Cuando te conocí
  mi alma cantó.
No hay como el
  momento en que
  muere la tarde.
Sangre desplomada
  contra la muralla
  que avanza
Por donde me encuentro
  y con quien ande
  estarás en el respiro.
Triste eras cuando te conocí.

TO R

Tu cara es como
          la luna llena.
Eres la tierra de mi querencia,
          triste y oscura al caer la lluvia.
Tus ojos siempre están al punto de llorar
          y tu boca es el
          lago hacia donde corre la luz.
¿Has visto el venado a punto de huir?
          Es tu cuerpo
Eres la pulpa y gabazo
          de los días.

TO R

Que diferencia cuando estás.
          cual momento
Cuando de repente llegas,
Todo se alumbra.

Y sea cual hora, el día comienza.
Ah sutil vestidora de alegrías, viento
          de perfumes
Presencia de sonrisas, quédate.
Tu voz campanilla de comunión.
          es música de baile.

Suave hada que tocas almas
Todo lo vuelves bueno.
Que no pase del encierro de mí,
          tu fiesta.
Ah tú que fuiste fiesta de mi vida.

Has dejado suave
          perfume de azucena.
Y sol alumbrado.

ORACIÓN

Divina flor que esparces bendiciones
Mira con gracia
Estas semillas pardas
Que, aunque no blancas,
Con la blancura del capullo
Guardan en sí, promesa del futuro
Y te alaban sin poesía
Rogando que no pongas condiciones.

Deja que tu belleza con nitidez de nácar
Y tu perfume, de esencia sin igual
Bendiga nuestra empresa
Nos dé máxima fuerza
Para alcanzar la meta de las luchas
Para saber lo que es la dignidad no a medias
Para vivir como hombre natural
Y nunca más dejarte de alabar.

A LA CHICANA

Ya la imagen perdida
Se quiebra como el vaso
No de alabastro o de cristal,
Sino de barro.
Y, tu tez besada por el sol

Como el capullo blanco
Interno, de tu ser paloma
Relumbra dando amor.

Y de la tierra madre, color
Dulce sabor
Sale a brindar
belleza y goce
perduración y fuerza
de la mujer Chicana.

LA NIEVE DE MINNESOTA

Flor de cielo
pura y blanda
capullo de cielo en flor.
Muerte salida de frío, mármol
sabe a hielo en cajilón.
Promesa de fino lino
manto de blanco invernal.
Cae la fría y dulce nieve
de cristal floresta vierte
en Minnesota tan lejos,
allá, tan lejos, allá.

IMAGEN DEL CAMPESINO

Como el terrón que bajo el sol
se desmorona
así el humilde piscador
de algodón, maíz o nueces
desvanece.
y bajo el incansable ojo de luz,
desamparado,
nos borra el vaho de la mañana
lo que despide el hombre:
Sudor y Sangre, Vida.

NOVEMBER 7, 1972

EN UN COMITÉ UNIVERSITARIO

Sentado en medio de "Los Grandes"
Tan rara la ocasión que aún me asombra
Y el derecho de estar, un poco así me estorba,
Porque al fin y al cabo algo tiene todo esto de "los pendes."

"Pendes" quiere decir, O,O,O, a la izquierda, que el sabio, entienda,
Cosa que no se dice aunque se sepa
Y toda la honradez más erudita
Calla, calla, y *tiembla,* aunque no diga nada.

Concilio es de torre amarfilada
Y *cierta dejadez, se nota en el vestir*
Como por despreciar lo mismo que se aprecia
Y ¿dónde está la realidad o fantasía?

Los viejos sabios oyen, mientras los jóvenes nos hablan,
Unos atentamente escuchan,
Otros se cansan
Y la mayoría, sin pensarlo, relajan.

Lo propuesto, palabras, a dónde llegarán,
Si muchos duermen dentro del papel que ellos nos dan,
Despierten jóvenes y no se gasten con tanto afán
Por todo aquello que los viejos les darán.

Pero al progreso hay que llegar, y como árboles verdes
Lograr que el alma
Sin cesar, siempre viva
Creciendo y adulando sus alcances.

JORGE GONZÁLEZ

BOGOTÁ

Tus estrechas calles
tus hermosos edificios
tus altares de oro
Bogotá
son opacos espejos
que bruman la miseria
de tu colonizada realidad

Por qué es que tu gente no sonríe
Bogotá
tus hombres
tus mujeres
tus niños
tienen hambre
Bogotá
tienen sed
tienen frío
velos
Bogotá
como luchan
por pesos sin valor
como roban
como matan
como aman
por respirar libres
de Lleras
de Rojas
de Gomes
de Pastrana
de toda esa camarilla
que con las manos
manchadas con sangre
de Jorge Elfécer Gaitán
de Camilo Torres Restrepo
de Efraín González
de incontables
patriotas colombianos
entregan
tus verdes esmeraldas
tu suave café
tus bananos
tu petróleo
TU GENTE
Y

TU DIGNIDAD
al yanqui
acaparador
mercante
de armas
y
muerte

¿QUÉ VAS A HACER
            BOGOTÁ?

MOMOSTENANGO

1
Una fresca mañana de aire limpio
los pinos erectos reflejaban mensajes solares con sus hojas
las campanas de la iglesia
llamaban a los fieles pobres a orar y a trabajar
un viejo labrador con su azadón al hombro marchaba decidido
su idéntico futuro lo seguía a limpiar el cementerio

2
Hasta el cementerio seguimos los pasos del pasado
y futuro en el presente
allí la comunidad labriega hablaba con los muertos
lloraba a la eternidad
en lo finito
la flama siempre viva
consumía cera y ahogaba a las flores

3
En la capilla de altares y paredes ennegrecidas
por el humo de la fe
un hombre con su canto pedía perdón
por sus inexistentes pecados
rascacielos de cera se consumían en el piso

perfume de copal desvanecía todo
                es un sueño

Victoria,
flor de mi derrota
de azules océanos
y conquistas medievales

renacida en Aztlán
acompañante de Quetzalcoatl
donde este y oeste se encontraron
tu sangre y la mía bañaron la tierra
hace mucho
en violenta guerra florida

el ciclo se completó
el sol brilla de noche
la luna de día
y el fruto de nuestra sangre
está por brotar en la tierra

Siempre en ese deseo inmediato
que niega por su existencia
todo hasta su herencia
encuentro mi alegretriste creencia
no de sabio
ni de santo
sino de poeta

MARÍA

Una lluvia de música
en mis oídos
cascadas eternas
de ritmos serpentinos
noche fresca
muchas lunas
una estrella solitaria
de amor supremo
boundless, boundless
like wings of light
like rays of sun
así te ví.

XOCHICALCO

El 21 de junio todo se alumbra:

Cavernas montañosas
cúspide de estrellas
sin sacrificio carnal
pa' los astros que con su luz-energía
en serpientes emplumadas nos llevan a otras galaxias

Xochicalco
flor enterrada
destinada a salir en poco tiempo
            espacio terrestre
pa' liberar el espíritu
del quinto sol deslumbrante
destinado en un instante
            a morir polvorizado

ANTIGUA

Nubes grises
cubren el sol de mediodía
la luz se polariza
las tranquilas calles
ahora están opacas:

Antigua
museo de tu realidad
tus cuarteadas cúpulas
no abrigan al destechado
pero sirven de nidos a los pájaros
tus omnipresentes escombros
no son abundantes milpas
pero cada piedra derivada conmemora tu creación

Antigua
eres el presente
el espejo de tu nación
eres música para el sordo
paisaje para el ciego
tu nacimiento te negó
por eso siemprevivos

13 septiembre, 1973

A SALVADOR ALLENDE

Valiente:
fusil en mano
compañero te enfrentaste
contra ejército tirano

bombas
tanques
balas
y morteros
atacaron La Moneda
con manos ensangrentadas
sedientas por el dinero

De suicidio también te acusan
con un balazo en la boca
pero nosotros sabemos
que te enfrentaste a la tropa

Los heroicos obreros
en parapetos situados
siguen luchando sin tregua
por tu ejemplo inspirados

La ola sigue creciendo
el ejército del pueblo
poco a poco es formado
con combatientes obreros
estudiantes progresistas
y campesinos valientes
se acerca la hora fija
de la victoria insurgente

Tu muerte compañero Allende
es lección del heroísmo
el derramar de tu sangre
nos muestra ese rojo vivo
de nuestra causa triunfante

Rojo, Rojo, Rojo y Rojo
en las estrellas y barras
en las banderas ondeantes
que tendrán todas las playas

¡Viva el Salvador Allende
mátir del pueblo chileno!
¡Vivan los trabajadores
que rehusan tener dueño!
¡Adelante para siempre
y siempre hasta la victoria!

AL TEATRO CAMPESINO

Mujeres oprimidas
por hombres oprimidos
dulzura amarga
de noches sin estrellas

Hombres oprimidos
por hombres oprimidos
campos ensangrentados
de sudor marchito
y espaldas deformadas

Plantamos, regamos y cosechamos el sustento
pero sólo las migajas comemos
construimos buenas casas
pero en ellas no vivimos
confeccionamos la ropa
blusas, vestidos, pantalones y calzones
pero en andrajos vestimos
hacemos huevos rancheros
los steaks y los pancakes,
los servimos, los platos se los lavamos
y de rodillas hasta el suelo nos fregamos
construimos ya las fábricas
y la abundancia creamos
construimos la nación
e hijos dimos al Pentagón

¡Pero basta ya compañeros!
¡compañeras y enemigos
comeremos la comida!
¡vestiremos esa ropa!
¡viviremos en las casas!
¡las fábricas serán nuestras!
¡la tierra será del pobre!
pues sean los trabajadores
Hombres mujeres o niños
dioses únicos han sido
hasta siempre lo serán
pues sólo ellos nos dan
que comer
que vestir
y hasta donde cantonear

Así es que hermanos y hermanas
no invoquen a dioses mitos
no brumen la realidad
nuestra vida está en la tierra
no se pierdan en el cielo
vámonos hacia la vida.

BARBARA HERNANDEZ

SING CHICANO SING

Through streets or pyramids lines with marcas on the wall

SING CHICANO SING

Through alleys sudados
     entre noches morenas
     sarapes coloriantes
     bajo sueños brillantes,

   !CANTA CHICANO CANTA!

Let your hands penetrate deep into the mother earth and let your
whole body breathe in the sweet aroma de la tierra húmeda,
     the sweet aromas de la tierra india,
     pecho rojo, Madre Tierra que nos arulle
     entre brazos quemados por fuego azteca
     que en nuestras venas corre.

!CANTA CHICANO CANTA!
  !POR LA RAZA CANTA!
   !POR LA LIBERACIÓN QUE PERSIGUES,
    !POR EL AMOR QUE BROTA DE EMOCIONES ROJAS!
    QUE BAILAN SOBRE OJAS DE OTOÑO, CANTA!

   !CANTA TU RENACIMIENTO, CANTA,
       QUE ERES
        CHICANO
        CANTA!

Once a dream did look upon a field of time,
only to discover it was alone;
it saw not the warmth of the sun;
it experienced neither the beauty of the stars,

For it had lost its path wandering among the shores of distant
moons and forgotten seas . . . .
it felt no pain;
it saw no hope;

it existed only in the dungeons of silence
 within corners of fear created by shattered emotions.

It cried tears of sorrow
 and developed thorns of emptiness,
  for it looked upon a field of time
   only to discover it was alone . . . . .

Chicanos

Organizing and socializing
Politicizing and sometimes materializing

Reading
   Writing
      Talking and yelling
         Singing
           Crying
              Working and slaving
                 Fighting and dying.

Vida loca
   Vida de Raza
      ¿Cuándo se acaba?

Brown brothers try to color themselves of a different shade
While fat mamas stand on the corner whistling a tune among
lonely shadows.

Sonny scores from Tiro;
Tiro sells to Chico;
Chico gives some to Gato y !ay se va!

PERO LA VIDA LOCA ¿CUÁNDO SE ACABA?

Chicanos, muy de aquellas, hacen organize y le hacen al socialize,
Pero, pues, ¿dónde está la materialize?

Pues, yo no sé nada de ese pedo,
Pero, I know that my people suffer
Everyday in the Barrio.

Y los carnalitos are siempre being hassled by the pigs.
Y también sé que mis jefitos trabajan in factories día y noche,
Noche y día, y todo ¿para qué?

¿Para qué sirve esta pinchi vida si hay que trabajar para darle todo
al gobierno mientras nos estamos muriendo de hambre?

!NO CAMARADA!

YA BASTA de organizing y socializing, politicizing y Mexanizing.

Las palabras se desaparecen con el viento y las acciones son las
que cuentan.

So carnal, vamos dejando de hablar y vamos poniéndonos a trabajar,
Que la lucha es dura
y los sufrimientos de la Raza son muchos!

JUAN FELIPE HERRERA

UNO

let us gather in a flourishing way
with sunluz grains abriendo los cantos
que cargamos cada día
en el young pasto nuestro cuerpo
para regalar y dar feliz perlas pearls
of corn flowing árboles de vida en las cuatro esquinas
let us gather in a flourishing way
contentos llenos de fuerza to vida
giving nacimientos to fragrant ríos
dulces frescos verdes turquoise strong
carne de nuestros hijos rainbows
let us gather in a flourishing way
en la luz y en la carne of our heart to toil
tranquilos in fields of blossoms
juntos to stretch los brazos
tranquilos with the rain en la mañana
temprana estrella on our forehead
cielo de calor and wisdom to meet us
where we toil seimpre
in the garden of our struggle and joy
let us offer our hearts a saludar our águila rising
freedom
a celebrar woven brazos branches ramas
piedras nopales plumas piercing bursting
figs and aguacates
ripe mariposa fields and mares claros
of our face
to breathe todos en el camino blessing
the seeds to give to grow maiztlán
en las manos de nuestro amor

DOS

rebozos of love
 we have woven
  sudor de pueblos
on our back

TRES

hace muchos años huichol
montañas ground maizitos red
plumas wrapped en bronce aquí
yo nací
para siembras y cantar
ruturi flor de la lira tuyamia
tamboras venado cuero
jorongo de la tierra diosa
siembra
para deep cantos cantas una
toda vida oval tauyepá sol
cara
tuyamia
enteros mil cuerpos
desnudos semilla fires
suben
de las sombras dark spiral sangre
secos
dry frías matas mares
las conchas campanas glow mi padre
tauyepá águilas sol
¿lo miras?
dark huipiles
lanos lana mugre carne
en el llano serpiente cara wrapped
odios
hechos a mano partida corazón
chupan la carnes frías entrañas sabores
maizita ciega
cáscaros hambras umbar alambres
de hambres en cielo sin sol
angustias tilichis mi
cuerpo miles of trenza rotas
siento las llamas latifundios
no brillan la vida
corazones huicholes
dragging feathers wilted
en mis guitarras milpas
el chapulinos se fue
no quiero
el mundo millas en carbón semillas murallas
dark estrollas
verdes
caras
sin ojos frutas hojas bloom mira
¡mira!
eres águila be born la luz
bendita rainbow
estambres caldos ground corn
jorongos jacaranas
trees pueblito frutos rico
canta huichol

zarape tejida fértil rebozos
frutos redondas sol ancho
amor tuyamia
flowing
forehands venas vengan woven sierras llenas
mariposas
tejuinos en la nochis quemando
ocote
rezas sudo
ocote humos mares
hirviendo espejos kindgom alas en tus trenzas
tuyomio
reino ground star corn of
quetzales creciendo un pueblo
cantas tamboros venado
spill chorros las sangres podrida
en el vientre del campos
selfmilpas no crecen
sacrificates el corazón&walk the sky jugos
radiant ground corn ombligo
abierta breathing dios rayos weaving
sol
amor
wisdom sudor
violeta red ground corn
entero pueblo to sprout

CUATRO

chapulines fly
 tierra sings
  rainbow trenza
we weave auroras

CINCO

sky
   en tus manos matutinas mundos
 hailing soles tu palabra
    the word que me dices como harpa y
 los coros eternos de tus risas
                    las ví
in the fountain of rainbows entre tus miradas
                        sí
    como un sol absoluta lumbre
      beso de luz
            lucero en la cumbre sky
          en la tierra flor de venus
              en tus manos matutinas
              conchas of love

SEIS

calavera del sol
 en tus brazos
  to live?
blow constellations

SIETE

mujer de sol ¿por qué estás triste?
                                        Y
¿por qué dejas tus cejas no canten esa canción
                    de la mañana que naciste
                flores dulces
        de las piedras negras y
                        uvas violetas con el calor de

                        amar?
                        mujer
        ¿sabes que aunque llores lloras un
                amanecer?

                            y las auroras en tu frente
            tejen espinas alas de una estrella
        ardor que ya no brilla
                y alumbran las siete rosas de tu ser
    songrise dawn
                mujer

OCHO

sunrise butterfly
besa al cielo
tierras
our forehead of light

NUEVE

come to frijol carnol y nala
IN A TOGETHER SOUPRAZA RISING
COME TO FRIJOL AND BLOOM GLOW
   BEING
AMERINDIAN FLUID sangres de dios
   liberate and flow again
tu caldo de luz frijol being so full

                        in tloque in nahuaque

come to frijol carnol y nala
   continENTE
      ASCENDIENTE

      YOUR labor of heart to

   wILL TO HUMANIZE

raza rise
   RAZAraíz egg of vibrant fibras IN A TOGETHER GLOW

in tloque in nahuaque dador de la vida in A TOGETHER
BLOOD FRIJOL BEING so full en tus entrañas

               amerindia being grows
               laborando
               cultivando
               in tloQUE IN NAHUAQUE
                  IN A TOGether souprazarisiNG. . .

DIEZ

            vamos a cantar
             dice el quetzal
             la luz del río
             our voice

ONCE

dawning luz
rosaluz
razaluz
brilla
our
path
we
blaze
our
heart
we
speak
lluvia
roja
fuente
song
of
struggle
song
of
tierra
song
of
sangres
song
of
fuego
raza
ahora
raza
llama
sean
los
pueblos
pueblos
flores
pueblos
libres
la
canción
la
semilla
el
corazón
de
la
nación
amerindia
amerindia
amerindia

sea
incandente
sea
consciente
living
sangres
living
tierra
living
árbol
amerindia
tree
of
heart
open
flower
divinacoatl
vereda
verdadera
flaming
eagles
voladores
tejedores
weaving
rings
cycles
spiral
space
spiral
time
of
our
heart
to
churn
burning
being
nuevo
ciclo
nuevo
espacio
nuevo
tiempo
consciente
dando
fruto

DOCE

corazón de venado
blaze of dawn walking
weave us a rain green
pa'l pueblo rojo
espigas humanas of roots
branching spirit
en un continente sin fin

TRECE

los grillos tocan sus acordiones
y los chapulines verdes vuelan
raspan sus cantos en el adobe

los campos brillan
la paja está cortada
los pinos crecen alto
el cedro y el piñón se mecen

corre el agua del ojo viejo
la mariposa y el cuervo
beben el sol y rajan al viento

"fíjese que antes era como si fuéramos
bendecidos por dios
se te caía una semilla y crecía una flor
los indios y nojotros teníamos fiesta juntos
bajábamos al río y cogíamo pescao
ahora señor
la gente ya no cree ya no cree
las sierras 'stán cercadas
y los rinches cobran pa' pescar en
nuestra mesma tierra que ya muy dura 'stá
que tenemo que hacer trabajo po' allá
en colorao en la mina o peleando los fuegos
en los bosques
antes el venadito venía pa'bajo del cerro
aca 'tras la casa corriendo libre alegre
'hora se necesita licencia pa' casar venao
por cincuenta dólares la hacen pos
nomás los texanos la compran
le digo señor era como si fuéramo bendecidos
por dios
ansina mero . . . . ."

los niños sus brazos castaños cargan leña
la piel de la mujer y el hombre es roja
apretada por el sol viva franca
salada y fecunda

"vamo' a ver
caminando sin platicar
laborando pa' encontrar nuestra vida
en este llano de soledad
vamo' hacer nuestra labor nuestra oración
el sacrificio sin ambición
caminando sin platicar en este llano
de pasto amarillo por el dolor
vamo' a ver
si vamo'a ser enteros ansina como el amanecer. . . ."

enteras y enteros corazón sin fronteras
hopi navajo san juan taos truchas chamisal
picurís pojoaque peñasco velarde amalia y
española piedra lumbre tres ritos las cruces
mesquite tierra amarilla santa fe y alburque
santa fuerza vamo'a ser

una luz una oración una labor una nación
la canción sin mirar o decir o medir la memoria
o el mañana
vamo'a ver

nuestros pueblos nuestros rostros y entrañas
soplar en el viento
murmurar en el río
palpitar en el llano
caminar sin platicar

una flor sin fronteras
en el pedregal

BRONCE

Yo soy de La Raza de Bronce
Y en mi corazón
Sólo crecen las flores de todas las
Culturas de paz.

Adoro los crepúsculos
              y el espíritu
                     de los Aztecas
Invade mi alma
Que se engalana.
Mi mente tiene recuerdos
              de lluvias
Que caen como manantiales en mil colores.
Los trinos de los pájaros
              hacen que mis sueños
                       de esta vida
Cabalguen a rienda suelta
              hacia
La ilusión iluminada por plateados y coloridos
                          cantares
                              que
Brotan como flores de mi alma
                siempre Indígena
Los campos
          y los olores
Hogareños aún, envuelven mi ser
                 con lo antiguo
De una magia familiar
              puedo reír con mis ojos
                     mas
Todo mi ser puede hablar sin decir palabra
                   pero más que nada
Puedo sentir el espíritu de mis hermanos
                 que me envuelve
En sentimientos de hermosura
Convirtiendo la tristeza
             en puras perlas repletas
De armonía y entendimiento.
Yo soy de La Raza de Bronce

ME HABLÓ

Yo soy Indígena
Acaso no siento la
Divina Madre Tierra
                    hablándome

¡Sí es claro! cada que tomo
Un manjar de su cuerpo
Mi conciencia en inocencia
                    preguntaba
¿Y yo qué te doy?

O es acaso mi Espíritu infantil
El que desea compasión hacia el
Trabajo de mis antepasados

Cuando tus esencias invaden
Mi camino y me hacen caminar
Por caminos con esencia a pinos
Y azares en botón, mi niñez
En sonrisas
                    preguntaba
¿Y yo qué te doy?

Más ayer sucedió
El golpecito en el corazón
Ella me contestó
                    disipando
La duda de mi alma

¿Y yo qué te doy?

Campanitas de suavidad
Así como la de los pajes
Alejaron mis remordimientos
Fue como si
            La Virgencita de Guadalupe
Hubiese dicho
                no es malo niña

Siempre y cuando no te olvides
En depositar las semillas de la
                        concepción
En el seno de la Madre Tierra

Así podrás disfrutar de su gran amor
Pídele a Tata Dios que su bendición
Esté sobre tus semillas y crecerán

Podrás siempre jugar con sus flores
Comer de sus manjares
                    Siempre hagas esto

Tú nunca das
             pero ya no preguntarás
Puesto que estos actos te pondrán
En armonía será como el principio
Puro deleite de estar viviendo
                    en amor.

ABSENCE

I was lonely.
My love has gone away.
My love kept burning
Like a great, great fire.

I whistled to the birds,
Asking them to go, swift,
Upon the winds
                    and
            find him.
They came back,
Bringing the most
Magnificent tones,
Filling my soul with music.

My love kept burning
Like a great, great fire.

I asked Jesus
To please pray
                    to our heavenly
Father
And bring him back.
Jesus came, bringing
Soft dreams to my spirit,
Making my soul understand
                            departure,
Filling my soul
                    with thanksgiving
To God
And singing with joy.

My love kept burning
Like a great, great fire.

I went to the flowers
And asked the petals
If he loved me so,
Bringing my eyes
And my spirit
Thousands of
            colors
In the company of
Millions of
            intoxicating scents.

My love kept burning
Like a great, great fire.

I went to the trees,
Asking them, if they
                    had seen him.
To please mark the way,
Bringing shadow

If there was sun
Upon my path,
Giving fruits of
                    countless
                            shapes
And billions of
Tastes and flavoring
                            juices
That filtered my being
Restoring my organs.

My love kept burning
Like a great, great fire.

I went to the water,
Asking if the flavor
                            of his lips
Were still upon her fountains,
                                    bringing
To my being
Showers like diamonds,
Unquenchable thirst,
Rainbows of enchanting
                            colors
And
Crystal clear dreams
Pointing to a future full of
Fertilizing gardens.

My love kept burning
Like a great, great fire.

I asked the winds
To bring him back
Upon their soft
                    breezes
And his warm arms
Around me
                    once again,
Bringing with them
Fresh breezes that
                            cleanse my body,
And making my limbs
Free of fatigue
                    and
Playing with my hair,
Making my spirit

                            feel
                                like a
                                    bird in
                                        flight.
My love keeps burning
Like a great, great fire.

ENRIQUE LAMADRID

THE HUNT

sun slips through where sky was stabbed and bleeding,
      celestial radiant wound of morning.
deer still linger at edges of shadows and darkness wanes.
with all the force of habit, the hunt begins.
      scattered shots perforate the dawn.
silence is razed. death is waged with shoulder cannons
      rendering lethal the hunter's gaze:
sight and slaughter, vision of oozing empty guts
slung from trees with ravens all around,
the hoofless carcasses hanging back in town
      frozen to the wind.

I also pick up arms, not knowing how it feels
      to put a bullet through a deer.
but they have fled this bleeding mountain,
      tails and noses in the wind.
everywhere we walk, screaming jays announce our presence,
calling out the warning. at midday I give up the hunt
for the dream, being content only to roam free
following deer trails away wherever they lead me.

hungry now, I lie down among grasses of time, blunt mesas
      bending pliant in the wind.
above, the sky's blue caldera swallows birds, wind,
      sun, and mountaintops as I gaze from
one horizon to another on the limits of the knowable known.
by day's end the vision is blurred. real targets
      turn wooden, mocking the game.
stumps with branches become ghostly bucks with twilight
      and the sun sets in a pool of blood.

we all return empty handed, a reluctant brotherhood
around a hunter's fire, not even a rabbit for our pot.
so we eat tortillas and drink coffee and begin to crave
that venison we had sought, thinking our hunger
      was honest and would bring us luck tomorrow.

behind us the moon rises in a flurry of shooting stars.
Orion watches with his dogs and bow.
      we send him our prayers,
hoping he will lend us his arrows
      and grant us some meat.

up in a lemon tree
stealing its fruit
amidst its heady scent
   and shiny leaves in
   subtle shades of green
   and yellow
telling the fruit from
   the foilage
feeling safe as a sloth
off the ground with
   plenty to hang onto
and even more to pluck
we felt like we were
getting away with it all
or that we owed the tree
   something
when a branch reached out
   with its thorns
and drew your blood

LANDMARK

it was only a large tree
rooted in lava boulders
   deep in a gorge

we sat across a river
from it as you sketched
   and I fell asleep

the sun was high the shadows
never reached us, till now

it was the only ponderosa
in miles of rolling sage
   and steep canyons
even with eyes shut could we
   feel its presence

it stands now transplanted
to another mental canyon
where the sun is almost
   a different color
I take refuge in the branches
   like a squirrel

and gaze up into the familiar
   cliffs, inside behind

CABRESTO LAKE

having stood
   their ground
giant barkless
   firs rise.
wooden phantoms
from out of the
   pale lake
their drowned
   branches
reach into moon-
   light
a gust of wind
   shakes loose
a shower of meteors
from the topmost
   naked limbs

PETROGLYPHS OF THE RÍO POÑIL DEL NORTE

to watch the pulses within the eye
of a wounded deer, the death dilations,
the pained contractions as to imagined
   bursts of light

is like watching the universe
   regarding itself

rings within watery rings
the way any bit of water will
   when disturbed
the way trees and bones grow
   in annular waves
   upon themselves
the way that pale band of rainbow
   always forms around a full
   moon behind clouds

that same centering of every bud,
   flower, breast, and mind

in every side canyon
in all the special places
there are carvings on the sandstone walls
   circles within circles within circles
some with mouths, some with hands and eyes,
others carried on the backs of running deer
   past groups of dancing people

FAR AWAY FROM AZTLÁN

Omeyocan
is the thirteenth heaven
of the Aztecs
and home of
Ometecuhtli and Omecihuatl,
Lord and Lady of Our Sustenance,
who gave birth to
their eternally warring children:
Quetzalcoatl,
god of life,
Creator of man,
Lord of the House of Dawn;
and Tezcatlipoca,
omnipotent god of darkness,
sorcerers, highwaymen,
Lord of the House of Night.

In this land
the Lord of the House of Night
has grown fat
at the Feast of the Flaying of Men.
Although I have never been there,
I carry within myself
my own Sal Si Puedes,
my own Siete Infiernos,
and I have wandered far from Aztlán.

For the Aztecs, the blue Tezcatlipoca
showed the way south;
Tonatiuh pointed east
and Quetzalcoatl led
the way west towards the sun.
the black Tezcatlipoca,
Lord of the House of Night,
held sway over the north.
It is not these sure directions
from place to place
but rather the clumsy leap,
the crooked inner flight
from uncertainty to uncertainty,
which writes the poetry of my life
in the book of Everyman.
We try hard
to become worthy
of the Lord of the House of Dawn.

Clowns, side show barkers,
high wire artists,
sellers of popcorn and cotton candy,
we travel with the circus
on back roads through country towns.
You can hear the creaking wheels
of our caravan and see the dust
when we set up our tents.
There is always one more show
and we are still
far away from Aztlán.

SPIRIT SONG

The Wintu tribe
has a spirit song
that says
all the universe
is the place for my hair.
So I send forth
strands of light
soaring through space
to catch all the world
in a playful glare.
With the Totonacs
I look up and smile.
A conspiracy of stars
dances towards the dawn.
I try to remember
the forgotten language
of the sun.

The mountain splits
in half and the past
rises through the gap
with his old owl's eyes
open wide and wing
beating hard against
what was and is
and towards the still to be.
Beneath the earth
fallen warriors sing.
At Tenenexpan,
Remojadas and Los Cerros
the laughing gods
turn tears to mirth.
There is no beginning
and all death is birth.

REFLECTIONS IN THE DESERT

The lizard reigns
grey and green

silence perched
on lava rock

He flicks a black tongue
and stares through me
with the coldness
of all his kin

Memory turns to vapor
loses color

is gone

Sand and saguaro
go up in heat waves

gone

I seek fountains
terraced gardens
blue forests
satyrs, nymphs
and the unicorn

A crow
wings above

Do I hear
a woman's moan?

Green lord
of death
and parched bone,
the lizard
ignores me
from his throne.

LANDSCAPE

Clouds of ivory hue
tinge the surface
of a Spanish sky,
there to burst and fall
in Mozarabic light,
a fountain spray
beneath an Andaluz sun
caught in some Alhambran
garden of my mind.

Gypsy moths
devour the curved glow
of an African afternoon
and a dark muezzin
calls down
the Moorish night.
Golden Age ballads
and a song
in praise of wine
by Samuel Ha-Nagid
drift through
the olive trees
towards the sea.

JUANA LA LOCA I

Juana
que estaba loca
llevaba el ataúd
del cuerpo de Felipe
por muchos años.

Y tú
que no estás loca
¿cómo vas a llevar
el recuerdo mío
cuando te dejo?

JUANA LA LOCA II

Ella sabía
que sin Felipe
el agua se haría negra,
sucio el aire,
y la siembra se moriría
en el campo.

¿Quién
la iba a creer
en aquel entonces?
Hace quinientos años.
Todos pensaban
que estaba loca.

JOANNA THE MAD I

Joanna
who was mad
carried Philip's body
in its coffin
for years.

You
who are not mad
how shall you carry
my memory
when I leave?

JOANNA THE MAD II

She knew
that without Philip
the water would turn black,
the air become foul,
the crops would die
in the fields.

Who
would believe her?
That was
five hundred years ago.
Everyone thought
she was crazy then.

FOR MARÍA

I came empty to the bar.
She talked to me of trips to Turkey,
a fire spun jar
which she subjected to her will to be,
some hardened, round, incarnate impossible
to mar once done substance of herself
curved back round to what the heart
holds dear in a cracked and chipped world:
we are what we are.
I drink myself through night towards day
and try to chisel words into warmth, fire
against this winter's cold.
She is a potter with her pots of clay,
cocktail waitress with kind words for lonely drunks
who stumble in, freezing from the dark,
having found no heat from a faint and fading star.
I think she has been to the end of the rainbow
and has seen the pot of gold.

SEEN AND OVERHEARD IN A CHICANO BAR

"Richie, have you got a minute.
Listen, man, karate is an *art, ese;*
it's not only the *body,* it's the *mind.*"
Meanwhile in the corner of the bar
the couple remind me
of playful apes I have seen in the zoo.
They are both pointing out
curiosities of each other's chest.
Now he leans and kisses.
She giggles,
half in delight, half in surprise.
They both get up
and leave together.
"Give me six months, *ese,*
I'll take almost any *bato;*
I don't care how big he is
because it's the *mind, ese,*
not just the *body.*"
That's the pity, *bato,*
la chavala you would like to make
has already gone
out the back door
with the guy you imagine
that with training
you'll be able to take.

ON A CAN OF COORS BEER IN A CHICANO BAR

On a can of Coors Beer
(brewed in Golden, Colorado)
look carefully
at the Pure Rocky Mountain Spring Water emblem,
and you will see to the right of the Spring
the face of Don Quijote,
and to his right the faint image of Sancho.

Don Quijote and Sancho look very old.
Viejitos from northern New México, southern Colorado.
The spring forms a white shawl,
un rebozo blanco
wrapped around the old knight's stooped shoulders,
midriff and scraggly legs.

El Caballero de la Triste Figura
and his faithful squire
are being pursued by a lion
and they advance cautiously
pero adelante y con valor
towards another lion

which awaits them with the claws of destiny
just beyond the oval
of their present moment of uncertainty.

The Banquet emblem hovers
above the heads of Don Quijote and Sancho.
It is red like the setting sun and beckons
más allá, un poco más allá.

The Banquet
is always *un poco más allá.*

These thoughts occur
in a Chicano bar
where gold is the color of dreams,
of beer and urine,
of medals for dead heroes,
of wealth given away or stolen,

of a splendid generosity
turned on itself
to give the very last, what is not drained
by fighting, shootings, and stabbings,
to the self, and to even give that away

Götterdammerung of the people of the sun,
which calls for a draft of beer
and another, and another, and another,
which calls for Darío's promise.
Esperamos el alba de oro.
We work, play, and feel our way towards that golden dawn.

ON SIGNING AN AGREEMENT TO READ POETRY
AT A STATE UNIVERSITY

Great state university,
and all your sage administrators,
you and I do enter into solemn covenant.
I swear I will not bring down on you
labor difficulties, strikes, civil tumults,
wars and epidemics. Neither will I
interrupt or delay transportation service,
nor use salacious, abusive or obscene language,
nor make obscene or offensive
movements or gestures.

If, however, it should happen
that, during the reading,
the IWW musters its strength
and that One Great Big Union
should call the last General Strike
of all the workers of the world,
and if, at the same time, Yeat's great Beast
slouches towards Bethlehem to be born
amidst floods, earthquakes, tornadoes,
civil wars, and dancing in the streets,
then, yea I say unto you as it is written,
that Article 3 of the Lecture Agreement and Clause 17
of the Standard Entertainment Contract Rider
shall be fulfilled. You won't owe me a cent
and I won't try to collect.
If we find ourselves, afterwards,
leaving town on the same fast train,
I won't look at you
and don't you look at me.

sunny afternoon
cool breeze
waves of enchantment
calling, beckoning, breaking.
on the edge of a cliff
a ray of light
shimmering reflecting
celestial motion
centrifugal force
the current of the wind
carrying the seagull
waves pounding
suds remain
not forever. . .

estoy en jardines
flores y corazones
lugar de un paraíso
una gloria
llena de alegría
en este sitio de misterio
lleno de presentimiento
camino delicado
encuentro flores
una no puedo dejar ir
¿cómo pudiera?
no la dejaré.
camino delicado
no deseo
ni pisar
flores churidas
en este sitio de misterio
verdaderamente son vidas.

yo contemplo
con tu presencia
¿caerán las hojas
de los árboles
lo mismo?
yo contemplo
¿los pájaros
chiflarían
lo mismo?
la sombra
mi ser
¿podría ser?
yo contemplo
con tu presencia

117

my reflection
          an offering of the flesh
looking mirror
          for a son of a bitch
a trance, a spell
          a dream within my life
unfolding roads
          of my life-style
spiritual inspirations
          of a rebellious soul
listen to its cries
          how it murmurs
a deliberate action
          of my beliefs
a nutshell of slavery
          in my destiny
an instant
                    that my soul captivated

                                        mirada de espinas
                                        mirada clavada
                                        sin amor no hay nada
                                        pero ¿cuándo no hay amor?
                                        duda y crisis
                                        en vano
                                        madres en llanto
                                        hermanos confundidos
                                        mundos en guerras
                                        la realidad
                                        estoy lleno de amargura
                                        la hipocresía
                                        una para mí
                                        otra para ti
                                        riéndonos de ella
                                        carcajadas de pendejos
                                        ¿qué podemos hacer?
                                        debemos de excomunicarnos
                                        pa'que hacer algo
                                        brindo a lo inútil
                                        vida hueca, vacía
                                        no me arrepiento de nada
                                        no más hay una vida que vivir
                                        mirada de espinas
                                        mirada clavada

para soñar,
para eso sirven
las ilusiones.
en realidad:
la tristeza,
la melancolía
por no obtener
la ilusión.
quisiera tener flores
para siempre,
de esas bonitas
que apenas están brotando.
quisiera tener. . .
piedras bonitas,
redondas, puntadas,
no importa,
piedras bonitas,
que melancolía,
que tristeza,
no obtener
la fugitiva ilusión.

if you can see me,
under the tree,
look at me.
I am,
as you are,
surrounded by demons,
devils with pitchforks
disguised in blue uniforms
silhouetted in cemented streets,
surrounded by walls. . .
the flames of hell,
fire melting flesh,
angels playing their harps,
struggling for peace
while I burn by the second.

cuando yo no era nada
los muertos resucitaban
no importa lo que digan
toda mi vida ha estado así
cuando yo no era nada
los varios muertos
los hijos sin padres
los quiero tanto
corazones palpitan
muertos gritan
renunciando el sueño
para mí
cualquier muerto
vive

When i die,
will i have done everything?
certainly i will have died.
feel the various breathing,
the lungs tied
knotting, ready to. . .
possess the body
how much longer?
how is one to die?
how is it possible?
curse, coincidence
how could it be?
how?
how?
i died 10,000 times
i feel alive,
like a 10,000 lb. stone
had just been lifted from my chest.

JOSÉ MONTOYA

FACES AT THE FIRST FARMWORKERS CONSTITUTIONAL CONVENTION

Just the other day
In Fresno,
In a giant arena
Architectured
To reject the very poor,
César Chávez brought
The very poor
Together
In large numbers.

Cuatrocientos delegados
On the convention floor
Alone
And a few
Thousand more
In the galleries—

And outside
(. . . ¡parecía el mercado de Toluca!)

The very poor had come
Together
For protection—

Thousands
From the chaos
Of past shameful harvests,
Culminating
That humble man's
Awesome task
Of organizing
The unorganizables!

Farmworkers!
(Workers of the fields!)

Campesinos!
(¡Peones de los campos de labores!)

Not lifeless executives.
Not, stranger yet,
Pompous politicians!

What I saw
Were the familiar
Faces
Of yester grapes
And labor camps,

Body dragging faces
Baked in the oven
Valle de Coachella
And frost-blistered
En las heladas de Sanger
During pruning time.

Faces that have
Dealt with
Exploiters and
Deporters
Y con contratistas
Chuecos.

Faces!

Faces black
From Florida with love
And Coca Cola

Y Raza
De Chicago
Brown Brown
Y de Tejas
Y Árabes de Lamont
Y así gente
That had come
From all the fields
Of all the farmlands
Of America.

Farmworkers!
Campesinos!
The very poor!

The unorganizables—
Now, at a convention!

Yet,
No fancy vinyl-covered
Briefcases here,
No Samsonite luggage
Nor Botany 500s,
Sólo ropa del trabajo
Pero bien planchadita
Y portafolios sencillos
De cartón
Y cada quien con su
Mochilita

Y taquitos
En el parking lot

Where old acquaintances
Renew friendships
And compare the
Different experiences
Of late

No longer merely
Comparing wages and
Camp conditions like
Before. . .
        (. . .¿a cuánto andan pagando
        pa' ya pa' la costa?)

New queries now, reflecting
The different experiences
Of late. . .
        (. . .and how many times were
        you arrested, brother?)

And the talk of the market
Place continues
And they listen to
Boastful, seasoned travelers
Who have left, for the time
Being at least,
The well-worn routes
Of the harvest-followers
And they talk of
Strange sounding places. . .
        (. . .pos sabe que yo andaba
        en el boicateo pa' ya pa'
        Filadelfia.)

The talk of the market place,
Reflecting the different
Experiences of late. . .

The talk of the market place
The parking place
The market lot
The parking lot
Where the families
Were bedded down
For three days
Amidst amistad
Y canciones

Canciones y más canciones

Singing de colores,
About solidaridad
Pa' siempre

And we shall overcome
En español

Singing, singing

Even inside
On that floor of decorum
Singing
In defiance
Of Mr. Roberts' own rules!

Singing

Singing and joking

       (. . . el que no esté de acuerdo
       con mi moción, que me la apele!)

Ca Ca car ca ja ja das
and table pounding
Belly rolls

Then

Earnestly, without embarrassment,
Back to work.

Faces!

Faces de farmworkers—
Organized!
Confident!
Unafraid!

Resoluteness
Without impudence—

       (. . .me dispensa hermano director,
       pero mi gente no ha comido.)

Faces!

Faces de campesinos,
Faces of the very poor
Confident,
Unafraid—

The unorganizable,
The people of the earth—
Today
Very seriously
Contemplating
The ratification
Of Article 37
For history
And forever!

DORINDA MORENO

SOUNDS OF SADNESS, SOUNDS OF SORROW, SOUNDS OF STRENGTH. These have been the forces that have motivated the activism of la mujer de hoy. Una viejita, a powerful woman that influenced my life, era mi abuela, Navajo. She would croon to me a vibrating chant, a sound of tenderness which still tremors through me today.

Su arullo de ternura sounds like this:

A ra ru ru ru   A ra ru ru ru   A ra ru ru ru   A ra ru-u-u

Mi abuelita también me contaba de la angustia de una madre desesperada. *"La llorona,"* she would say, "killed her children because she did not have any food to feed them." Her llanto, her pena, would send a chill through the night, causing even grown men to tremble. En la noche, especially down by the river, it's not the wind; it's *la llorona* wailing a cry of agony, forever cursed, searching in vain for her children!

That sound of sadness goes like this:

"H i j o o o s!   P o b r e s   M i s   H i j o o s!

H i j o o s!   P o b r e c i t o s   M i s   H i j o s !"

There are still many children who die of starvation because they do not have any food in their bellies, but no longer does a woman have to suffer this anguish in total resignation. No longer a woman watch her children die a slow death, while she remains silent. Unlike the *llorona* and her act of futility, ACTIVISM has brought about a new dimension of la mujer.

Militancy has resurged. In Silver City, Nuevo México, in the land of my grandmother . . . where my father worked the copper mines . . . a new force has resounded. Dolores Revueltas symbolized the awakening and the strengthening of "el movimiento" with the fuerza and the participación of la mujer in the miners' strike. The women brought *la familia* into the struggle and onto victory.

From this heroic stand of rebeldía, of courage, the spirit of la nueva Chicana was proclaimed.

The sound of strength goes like this:

QUIEREMOS PAN
QUIEREMOS TRABAJOS
QUIEREMOS ORGANIZACIÓN
QUIEREMOS UFWOC
QUIEREMOS LA FORMULA
QUIERMOS J U S T I C I A!!

"LA MUJER   —   EN PIE DE LUCHA: ¡¡Y LA HORA ES YA!   125

O CALIFORNIA

se fueron
por el camino real
ese largo y triste camino de eucaliptos
en carretas con burros
un montón de frijol y maíz
y llegaron en lowered down chevys
with gafas fileros
speaking about the low life
tomando botellas de tequila
que decían Made in México
hablando tres palabras de inglés
apple pie y coffee
cantando
Vámonos a California
Vámonos a California

se iban
por el alambre
indios de calzón blanco y huarache
y aterrizaban
pochos pachucos perdidos
vatos locos con tatuajes mágicos
de vida y muerte
esperando en las esquinas el big hit
the 5 & 10 of caliente race track
that never came
cantando calladitos por las calles iban
Vámonos a California
Vámonos a California

they came
from New York
New York the big apple
to the big orange
Yorubas Jíbaros Borinquens
regando las calles con bacardí
piel color café oscuro
ojos de verde cocodrilo
y un tun-tun de tambores
de viejas selvas ancestrales
que alguna vez fueron
pero ahora con mil memorias
de viajes mal pagados
Vámonos a California
Vámonos a California
Vámonos a California

CANTO DEL ROJO Y NEGRO

ojos de obsidiano
mantel de lino
cuarto de cuatro ventanas
lluvia sobre el pueblo
sol sobre las nubes

todo pasa
todo cambia lo que fue a
lo que fue alguna vez
otra vez será
lo bueno de un día
será lo malo de la misma noche
la canción de hoy
es el llanto de mañana
todo pasa
todo cambia

las cosas se hacen
las heridas se cierran
pueblos arazados
alguna vez se levantarán
ojos hinchados
alguna vez se van a secar
como un río seco
volverá a correr
pa' regresar como agua del cielo

un amor de este tiempo
es el amor de la vida pasada
así decían las escrituras
de los ancianos hombres
hechos de maíz
sabiendo que sus
cuerpos también regresarán
como las pirámides de teotihuacán
como monte albán
el sentido de vida de otros tiempos
será otra vez más
como copán
escribían los ancianos
que uno tiene muchas vidas
pero no más una sola alma.

Todo es uno
uno es todo
lo que por la luz es malo
será bueno por las sombras
soldados hoy
ayer fueron campesinos
libres ayer
ahora presos
los de arriba
son los de abajo
el círculo de los siglos

el círculo de los siglos
subirá los de abajo
y derrotará los de arriba

todo cambia
todo pasa
la lluvia se quiebra sobre los cerros
luna se mete a las nubes
cuarto de cuatro puertas
mantel de lino
ojos de obsidiano.

SWEET SOLEDAD

clouds raced across the sky as so many buffalos
in the plains of yesterday sweet solitudes
waiting for us at the end of a thousand days
when you said my name to the echo of night the
long trumpet of loneliness sounded back/ i was
gone searching across northern deserts for the flower
that blooms at mid-night sweet solitudes
waiting at the train station for your omnipresent
homecoming. a band of vagabond beggars struck
up the chorus of destitution on the pavement a
single blade of grass burst thru ending the
regime of the concrete ones/ ending the spell of
the plastic ministers that ruled the mind but not
the soul sweet solitudes and you.

when there was us. passing time from hand to
hand old bottles empty glasses sorry memories of saturday
that were such bad movies of our lives they would
have played nowhere. pessimistic lovers entren-
ched upon a wooden cross of unemployment bad
checks and welfare stamps that were a poor excuse
for life. long lines at the door waiting for the
big break to come inside/ sweet solitudes made of
us. a handful of words a sentence or two a story that one of us got
started on and wound up bored or crying because the tale was too
long and time so short and sweet solitudes made of two.
of me and of you.

el tecato sits back, he lights a frajo
he takes out his ere
he prepares his chiva
an expert at his trade
at what he lives for
que viva la vida loca for another day
que viva el sueño
que viva el tecato for another day
so he can buy his pleasure
from the local street pusher
que viva el local pusher
who struggles to survive
la vida, this life
que viva el bigger pusher
up the line
que viva ese pusher
who also just seeks to survive
que visa su provider
who is just making a living

el mero chingón sits back
con las patas pa'rriba
se hecha un pedo
y todos a rodillas
él es el mero mero
él es el más cabrón
él es el más chingón
él es que lo hace for la feria
él es que pasa sus leyes
to protect his interest
his money
his chiva
his heroin, his heroin, his heroin, his heroin
his carga, his carga, his carga, his carga
his cargo of money
his cargo of heroin
his cargo of death

el estudiante y el tecato are one
they are both addicts
support one pusher
depend on one system
to provide them with their needs
one with chiva and the other with feria
they are both addicts to the system
both hooked up directly to the system
one with his arteries
the other with his mind
one physically hooked and the other mentally
hooked
they are both brothers
both are innocent of what they are
both act in their own ways
both act on each other
argue with each other
kill each other
los dos son locos
uno se pone loco el otro se vuelve loco
los dos son filósofos "uno para él solo"
                              "el otro pa'el pueblo"
both seek liberation
one to liberate his body of the chango
of the gusanos under his skin
he needs chiva he needs money
he knows what he needs
he knows what it takes
it is for real

el estudiante sits back con sus patas pa'rriba
his eyes in a book and his head in his ass
he reads on, on, on, and on
he becomes as they say politicized
he becomes as they say aware of the oppression of his people
he survives on his parents' money
on EOP aid
on work study
on the systema
for his job, for his jobs,
he is also a histler,
he knows how to read,
he knows how to talk,
how to read, how to talk, how to read, how to talk, how to read, how to talk
a new vocabulary he learns to articulate.
he reacts blindly to the loss of his chupón, of his chupón
he reacts sharply to his own carnal,
upon his own brother,
brown, black, yellow, Brother,
on his brother, trying to survive,
he made it why shouldn't you
you have to try,
you have to work,
for the system who feeds you, who owns you, who turns you on and turns you off
so you can buy his food, pay his rent, buy his new car, buy his gas

support his habit profit
it is life or it is death
it is the systema
The other seeks liberation too
he finds confusion
he wants to get his shit together
to do what is right
for his carnal
comunista, marxista, leninista, trotskysta, nacionalista, culturista
palabras, words, confusion, talk
fight each other
blow each others minds
call each other names
play games
play games
play games with each other with each other people
tic tac toe
philosophize, intellectualize, talk, rhetoric, words
qué pasó, qué estás haciendo, 'ónde vas, 'ónde vamos
qué dices, no te entiendo
I don't understand what comes from your boca
are you on acid or algo?
am i on acid or something?
bullshit you are, estás loco y no un poco
get out of here, split, I may be ignorant but I am not crazy
descuéntate o te descontamos, we'll call the pigs on you, so a volar
esos vatos del colegio están destrampados, they must have it hard
Moscas come and moscas go
new ideas, ideologies, philosophies, incoherent, sounds only talk
pura cábula pero no acción etc., etc., etc.

tecatos become and tecatos die, innocent live innocent die, pura cábula y no
    acción
y moscas come and moscas go
one who gets drunk on thought
even though he may drink
and is not an alcoholic
he does get drunk

eventhough we live in the monster
our stomach is full
but our minds are empty
raza must liberate their spirits from las cadenas
si los veteranos
si los veteranos leaders
of our tribe xicano
without blood leadership
have cut a path
a path for la raza
decides to sit back
to take some fruit because it is his path
then carnal, don't sit back too long
the path needs clearing
thorns grow because of envidia
because you know what is happening

because it's yours and no one else
step aside, sober up
when you are ready the path will be ready
The time is now
panahon na

ANTONIO G. ORTÍZ

SACRAMENTO

In childhood I heard the
           Sunday slurp.
I saw the Ancient Ones standing
With empty pots and throbbing heads.
No one spoke
For who would break
The silence of communion?
This morning one paid for last night's sins:
Of lost wages
           Of found women
                      Of whatever.

Menudo was such a private sacrament
Made only to the gods of cruda.
A pinch of this,
A twig of that,
And everything was right.

How holy must have been those
           Ancient Ones,
For they never missed their
           Sunday slurp.

OCTOBER 1971

There is a void between the universe
Where lost light lives,
Where memories are frosted
With the dews of yesterday,
Where children live their lives in peace,
Where man has learned to love.
There is time to live
           in this unknown wilderness
For man is not afraid of man.
I tell you of this unseen world
And wish that you were here
For, when I passed it, many years ago,
I lost it in a tear.   133

PRISM PRISON

Tiny pinpoints dance
           like fireflies in the night:
Floating delicacies trying to
           weave and
       wave and
                   destroy themselves.
They change from white
           and sparkle into blue;
And now the cloud's a brilliant
           violet.

The lavender streaks toss among the
           golden springs.
Now, the blackness comes—
           but yellow fades it out.

Many times, in many ways
           the colors play their games.
I can't tint my mind;
           I can't streak my thoughts;
I can only flow into the prism
           that is Now.

MACHO

You spend a lifetime with a empty feeling,
And time never seems right.
You watch the seasons change their colors,
And the lonely hours creep by.
You talk with some,
           and laugh with others,
                   and your heart is filled
                           with sadness.
But your stubborn mind won't let the tears come.
You reach out for some warmth,
           and you're told to wait.

But for you the waiting time is gone,
           and you want the loneliness to be gone
                   now.
But someone else has their own time schedule,
           and is not willing
                   to change their mind.
How long will it be
           before the teardrops
                   change your mind?

HENRY PACHECO

in the fields
our family—

Los Braceros Norte' Americanos

calmly weed the green Colorado patches

row by row

in pace of gritty sun-clouds
following daughters, cousins
and the memory of my grandmother stricken
with the walking death.

La Muerte Andando!

I gather cucumbers and solar squinting
glances,
abilities of patience and sentiment,
and the other starch-sprout
workers.

Listen — those words come into my mind
nightly and by day (from time past time)
in a tongue lacking anything by soul
and strength. Not telling me all.

Leading me toward escape
they awaken voices of my kindred past—
when I was a boy and "Chicano" only.

I am nothing but a slight brown man:
a chipped tooth, curly black hair
a white eyebrow, a scarred hand
Short, skinny and white-legged
a flattened nose, a scar-streaked forehead
Gap-toothed and full-lipped
I worry about myself; late at night,
Realizing that my brother has died
—I plan a humble poet's disguise.

CANTO JUVENIL

Almas que brotan de su nidal,
cantan y despiertan.
Brillan los ojos al deslumbrar;
El pecho más respira, ansiosamente,
anticipando, su calor apasionado.

Y el encierro de sufrir, fue algo
que no se imaginó.
La sentencia de vivir, un amor
que nos trajo
para descrubrirnos, entre las mentiras,
y la facultad del ser que las perpetúa,
en Cuanto Juvenil.

Stillness crept into our hearts,
resounding to joyous dreams.
Echoes of silence lost,
return us to memories.
While we forget, who we've become,
Children with bright, laughing faces
remind us that the earth is still young,
is still being born.

AZTLÁN

Nadie te entiende
No lo pueden saber
No te comprenden
No lo pueden ver

Todo lo que sufres,
Dos vidas que has tenido que sostener
Los dos sentidos:
Realización de tu poder.

Esta es tu tierra
Todo se tendrá que devolver
Espíritu de fierro.
Así se realiza tu poder

Todo lo malo,
se tendrá que resolver;
entre tus manos,
y entre el esfuerzo de querer.

AZTLÁN, AZTLÁN

Tus niños, . . . te llaman:

AZTLÁN, . . . AZTLÁN!

LYNNE ROMERO

OLA TE SALUDO
OLA LUNA
OLA SOL
QUE SURGIMOS
DEL VIENTRE DE LA TIERRA
Y NOS TAPAMOS
CON ESPUMAS
DE AMOR
TIERNOS NOS
REFRESCAMOS
NOS MIRAMOS
NOS SALUDAMOS
OLA TE SALUDO YO

¿POR QUÉ ES QUE LA GENTE QUE VIVE CON LA TIERRA VE EL MAR LLORAR?

Baile sin luz
Corazón que no late
y piojos cuajados en mi lechón
Veo y no veo
Sé y no sé
¿Por qué?
la vida humana
ya no sabe lo que es
ser de sangre, ser de tierra
y respirar la luna
y deleitar un manjar
de rosas
y nixtamal
y hasta un gallo
tempranito en la mañana
que todavía no sale el sol.

Instrument of Peace
    through joyful penetration
Breathing deep from beneath
touching roots of ancestral souls.

To Speak your words of mind

Can you see them
through the haze of smoke
of true love and peace signs
When you get up and rise
mi Raza sí —
say it from your pecho
to me
see yourself in me
let your eyes shine
moon shine reflecting
clear water

Speak forth fire mouth
flames of anguish that cry Aztlán
New world to be seen by you and me
planting seeds from our breasts
hearts that speak forth
no words to hear only songs
to know your eyes in mine
 the barrio days of read and white and green
and maíz that grew and gallos early in the morning
reminding you of a new day with pan dulce with conchas
that bleed after rape
get up get out of bed
squeeze the piojos from your head
hmmm a soft blow to your mind
soften the fall
remember to rise
to spit and shout and dance and sing
try to forget   to forget? forget from when before
 there was always a ceremonia not to forget
in our eyes to know in our breasts the seeds to plant
in our heart our cry our fire mouth which burns and
shakes soothed by the sea which unites you and me
to a new world to be seen a world of us
Aztlán to be free

dejémonos deslizar
sobre llanos de antiguos parientes que conocemos
en nuestros ojos a mirar.
Conozcamos juntos las verdades y los cantares de un tiempo
que no debemos olvidar
Llanos verdes lagunas ondas que suspiran y murmuran
que nos alentan con ollas de barro y faldas de algodón
pintadas adornadas exclamando soy yo eres tú somos
seremos aquellos que den antes observaban respetaban
adoraban recordaban que la tierra no se trata mal
y que los luceros alumbran corazones que palpitan
con vientos que entran por grutas secretas de los llanos
de antiguos parientes que conocemos en nuestros ojos al
mirar.

Cuántas veces
nos hemos visto
sin mirar

nos
hemos mirado
sin hablar

nos hemos
hablado sin
sonar

Hemos visto la
gota de lluvia
el gato menear
y la música alzar

toca una voz
que suena sin
hablar

cuántas veces hemos
conocido dedos
al mirar y voces
al tocar

Cuántas veces
nos hemos
dejado reflejar

cinco vidas
       tres presos
            almas perdidas
                  carnes sin hueso
ametralladora usa
clavos para comer
cabinets everything
in its place
and the conductor
plays your pace

Por mi raza habla
mi espíritu
un espíritu estrujido
por las conformidades
y normalidades de
una vida envasada
y dictada por
máquinas
y series
de caras enlatadas
no deposit no
return
recycle your
air and try and make it
there - where?

to lagunas profundas
cielos y vapores de
mil colores
cantos alegres
rocíos de amores
verdes
luna sol tierra
Quetzal

Somos Raza
Chicharrones
Polvorones
Nopales
y Canciones

Remember your
masa cuajada
de manos
y pies
Tonatzin
Tlaloc
Tizoc
Hierbas plumas
colores
vapores
deer antlers
you dance
vidas you
blend

Por la fuerza
de mi Raza
Espíritu Luz
Nuevo Mundo A Crear
Vida Real
to disfrutar
Life Complete
Realizar
Your Raza
Being
- Sol

Cinco sagrado
        tres circulando
                Almas eternas
                     Vidas total
    Raza Bronce
        Sexto Sol A Brillar!

TO SISTERS

al bailar
hard to believe
quiet
heart speaks
espíritus de la tierra
ofrézcanme su bendición
               aaaaaayyyyyy watch out home girl
get out of my way
the moon was eclipsed as the butterfly blossomed
closeness and aliveness
        or do you say
chale!
there is only one way
and stop smiling
soul welfare of all
come home to feel good again
no more solution
you feel you have it
right now
closeness and aliveness
        tripping down the street
see the hermanita
uuuuuu so sweet
she walks near the moon
and venus close
stars in her eyes
her wings emerge and she flies
butterfly blossom soul awake
closeness and aliveness
        only was butterfly
emerging from cocoon
maybe too soon
it tore she fell

carnala tan chula
come home to feel good again
ahorita regreso
no llores mamacita
ahorita regreso
voy a buscar
donde me caí al mar
to feel good again
no more solution
you feel you have it
closeness and aliveness
                    eeeyyy
sock it to me
al bailar
sing your
life
¿por qué lloras mamacita?
no sabes que tu papito aquí te va cuidar
                    just look don't touch
that nasty prostitute she's good too
                    come home
to feel good again
no more solution
you feel you have it
right now
closeness and aliveness
                    aaayyy cabrona
como metiste la pata
ahora sí que las vas a tener que pagar
uuuy pos sí te va costar rete caro
pos fíjate nomás que no tiene precio
                    like bird sitting
on peach blossom
soon fruit
soon fly
                    get your wings on over here
and fly yeah
fly
all right
serpiente move softly over the earth
unos dicen you sinned
Quetzalcoatl
Kukulkan
                    hmmmmmm shake your self about
gather along the way
on your new skin
kisses of dew
ya no llores
ay mamacita ya no llores
ahorita regreso

Nuestra liberación
es iluminada
por nuestros espíritus
y corazones
guiados
por IN LAK 'ECH
    expresión Maya:
Tú Eres Mi Otro Yo
Y así el amor
y la fuerza
De Dios
el florecer
de la Raza
y el brillar
de Nuestro Sexto
Sol será

Our liberation
is illuminated
by our spirits
and hearts
guided
by IN LAK 'ECH
    a Maya expression:
You Are The Reflection of Me
In this way the love
and strength
Of God
the flowering
of the People
and the brilliance
of Our Sixth
Sun shall be

QUIXOTIC EXPECTATION

This day of quixotic
   expectation
      and lady like caution
         of clever mermaids
            in my basement

I am in an excitable
   nightingale parlor
      where troubled angels
         play cards

the sky is making noises
   my gypsy girl friend
      is drunk
   I am terribly angry

the world is aloof anyway
   filled with belly buttons
      and murders

last night's sex game
   was in keeping
      with my dogmatic
         religion

my frog soup diet
      is causing nightmares
   my eye doctor is insane
      rides a camel
      to work

the bride looks lovely anyway
      in her church bell mansion
   tongues hang in the wind
      and I've got to shout
         to be heard

Isn't it silly
   talking to an adding machine
      at three o'clock
         in the morning

AZTEC ANGEL

I

I am an Aztec angel
   criminal
      of a scholarly
         society
   I do favors
      for whimsical
         magicians
   where I pawn
   my heart
      for truth
   and find
      my way
   through obscure
      streets
      of soft spoken
         hara-kiris

II

I am an Aztec angel
   forlorn passenger
      on a train
   of chicken farmers
      and happy children

III

I am the Aztec angel
   fraternal partner
      of an orthodox
      society
   where pachuco children
      hurl stones
   through poetry rooms
and end up in a cop car
   their bones itching
      and their hearts
   busted from malnutrition

IV

I am the Aztec angel
   who frequents bars
spends evenings
      with literary circles
   and socializes
      with spiks
   niggers and wops
      and collapses on his way to
      to funerals

V

Drunk
lonely
bespectacled
the sky
opens my veins
like rain
clouds go berserk
around me
my Mexican ancestors
chew my fingernails
I am an Aztec angel
offspring
of a woman
who was beautiful

SUNDAY . . . DIG THE EMPTY SOUNDS

It is Sunday and I look for you
a meteor wandering, lazy,
simple as dust. I've encountered life here
a single shadow discovering the breast.
I bake the joys of afternoons in the sun,
with the blood of children
running weakly through the street
struck dumb by dark.

The human eyes of women loiter
here like stars on the cobblestones
water of the oppressed
standing still on the horizon
caught like a fish in the narrow heart
of mice. . .

The human mouths of clouds
go by here
running thieves in the sunlight.

I survive the rain
dreaming, lost, frowning
the shoes of my mother
talking
to the children in Africa
to the crazy dogs
that huddle in corners
starving
empty of sound.

                                        ASS

                    Yesterday
                        I thought
                            myself a prince
                                rode horseback
                                    beside a river

                    and fell on my ass
                    Walked beside her ladyship
                                and fell on my ass
                    the kingdom is talking
                                my kingdom
                    Salinas fell on his ass
                        on his way to mass

MEXICO AGE FOUR

I

on the corner to my house
is a churro factory
where the sweet tooth doubts
and the free man sleeps
how ugly the air smells in this town
as if torn hair and blood
were on the paving stones,
and taxi drivers asleep on their meters,
sluts
drink iced-tea through the shattered
windows
I see only
hungry beggars and sheep
on their knees

II

traveling through a cemetary in Saltillo
I find a truth as terrible as
murder
belly buttons and taciturn devils
paint the walls
of MEXICO
and I can no longer see pain
only the drip of the water
on a leaky rooftop

III

the dogs bark
at every doctor and at police
drunk
the moonlight gathers in the stoic
leaves of autumn

IV

and I take heaven as my ally
and sleep soundly
through the haunted
screams
of nights
as cold as mud
and
sighs of love
as deep
as pig grunts
silenced by their masters

I.

I am Omar
  the crazy gypsy
    nimble footed
      and carefree

    I write poems
      on walls
        that crumble
          and fall

    I talk to shadows
      that sleep
        and go away
          crying

    I meet fearless girls
      who tell me
        their troubles
          my loneliness
            bottled up in their
              tummy.

II.

I am Omar
  the crazy gypsy
    I write songs
      to my dead mother
        hurl stones
          at fat policemen
            and walk on seaweed
            in my dreams.

I walk away from despair
like a horse walks away
  from his master
    end up in jail
      eating powdered eggs
        for breakfast.

III.

My spine shakes
  to the songs
    of women

  I am heartless and lonely
    and I whistle a tune
      out of one of my dreams
        where the world
          babbles out loud
            and Mexican hat check girls
              do the Salinas Shuffle
            a dance composed
              by me in one
                of my nightmares
              and sold
            for a bottle
              of tequila.

IV.

I am Omar
  the crazy gypsy
    I waltz through avenues
      of roses
    to the song
      of Mariachis

V.

I am Omar
    the Mexican gypsy
. . . .
      I speak of love
        as something
      whimsical and aloof
        as something
      naked and cruel

I speak of death
      as something inhabiting
          the sea
        awkward and removed

I speak of hate
      as something
        nibbling my ear. . . .

RAÚLRSALINAS

HOMENAJE AL PACHUCO
(Mirrored Reflections)

¡Ese Loco. . .
      cúrate!
Dig on what/
   on what them dudes are saying,
      VATO.
That you are (¡ja-ja, que lucas!):
   a non-goal oriented,
     alienated being,
        sufriendo un "identity-crisis,"
rejecting conventional modes & mores.
   ¡Me La Rayo!

Y wacha,
   dizque you sprang from EL CHUCO,
Boogie'd into LOS
       & found
          the battleground
for US Naval wars;
   y se acá.
Orale, simón que sí.

But check THIZ/quiz OUT
   en l'escuelin:
      PACHUCO MYTHOLOGY – Room 1
      PACHUCO LANGUAGE
       Caló: Patois, Argot, or Jargon – Room 2
      THE PACHUCO AS A POP-HERO – Room 3
      PACHUCO: MISCREANT OR SOCIAL DEVIANT – Room 4
      PACHUCO PHILOSOPHY – Room 5
      THE PACHUCO AS A PACHUCO – Room 6

Isn't that far out?
   ¿Y la extensión/evolución?
      ¿A León?

As if to say
   (besides that your tramos were perhaps
      from Pachuca – en el terre – where
        campesinos wear piyama drapes)
that carnales: Pachucos/Vatos Locos/Low Riders/Yuvinales/
      Midgets/Juniors/Chavalones/Veteranos/Hipsters/
      Connección/Kin'pin-Machín/
    don't still fill
  las cárceles de Aztlán.

That brothers don't
    still walk the prison-yard
en FLORENCE/SANTA/FOLSOM/ & CAÑON
        (¿y la federal?)
Que no piscan algoda
    (grimme some alagodone, MESKIN)
en la TEJANA
    aquel animal tan horroroso.

As if to say that
    RAZA Blood
        does not continue flowing
on the GOD-DAMNED, gloomy streets
    of this Oppressive, Racist,
        Creativity-Stifling
            PINCHE SOCIEDAD!!!

That CARNATION didn't fall in QUENTIN,
    CAMELLO no quedó tasajeado en el Rancho HARLEM #1
        (or was it BLUE RIDGE Kamp?)
That MAMULA didn't drive
    bullet-riddled Buick
        into the heart of the barrio
    & died con cuete en mano
Que'l BOÑO de Watts
    isn't doing LIFE.

As if to add
    insult to injury,
one chump went on to say,
    you died a-borning!!!
        ¿Qui'ubo?
Pero lo mas sura was
    that in all their
        SOCIOLOGICAL
        ANTHROPOLOGICAL
        PSYCHOLOGICAL
        & HISTORICAL
heaps & piles of boguish bullshit,
    out sister—La Pachuca—of the
        equal sufrimientos;
aquella carnalita que también,
    who also bore the brunt
        de toda la carrilla;
remained in their textbooks
        ANONYMOUS.

So when you found
    his Mickey-Mouse world
        too A-bominable to accept,
you reject.
    What did he expect?
Pero ahí se va,
    no sweat,
        tú nomás juegala fría

& wait.
    Por tu resistencia perdurable
      someday
        he will grow tired
    & go away.

¿Cómo la ves tú, Compa?
    If we negate these further realities,
      ¡se salen!
Y le peleamos la causa al gringo
    that we're Not ahistorical.

Yet no mention
    que por esta pinche vida was
      SUFRIENDO.
Dibujos — TONANTZIN Y HUITZILOPOCHTLI — grabados,
    tatuajados en tu piel bronceada
      con las
        Ardientes Agujas
de esta gacha sociedad;
        que no sabe llorar
por niños hambrientos a migrantes sin trabajo.
    Much less give a damn, a good god-damn
      about
        street-corner born,
          forlorn fugitives
of the total jail
    Hail Pachuco!

SINFONÍA SERRANA

how can
i
sing you
songs of love

when all
i
ever learned were
howls of hate

i
cannot gift you
with
bouquets of joy

my
garden only yields
wild
weeds of sorrow

you
asked for the sun
i
could not provide

the
blame is not yours

i
wanted the moon
i
cried for the moon

when the
wrappings came off
i found
plastic and sham

so
to nurse both our
wounds from the
thorns of deceit

we
will sign our
last love-pact
in blood

with
the scalpel of loneliness
i'll carve you a sliver
of my soul

to
paste up in
the scrapbook
of your heart

even
tho'
i
know

poems
don't bring in
much money
these days

CANTO
(just for the hell of it)

Tú
  y
    Yo
      cucaracho. . .
parnas desde aquel entonces
          de
colchas calientitas   y
              veredas solitarias,
con 'buelita Mane
      y tía Mage.

Cuates desde los primeros años
      de abandono. . .
            nuestra huerfandad.

      "No tengo padre
      ni madre,
      ni un perrito
      que me ladre."

The first chingazos/
           cabronazos
Early slashes/
        gashes
from the piercing
      Knife
        of
          Life.

Escondidos/
        asustados
    en rincones de
      la cárcel del terror.
Después de largos (y amargos) años;
mountains de ladrío
    & rejas of steel
were pulverized/internalized/
            & CRYSTALIZED
(con ayuda de la voz de rebelión).
    We brewed that batch
      de vino dulce
for brothers/sisters/gente
    (thirsty people)
      to partake.

¿Y ahora, que haces aquí?
    UUUUUUU - NIIIIII -
             versitario!
¿Qué chingaos haces aquí . . . ?

con todos estos Ph.D's
spouting polyglot abstractions
(those nowhere distractions)
which we cannot CONceptualize.

Con la Mujer
            de ayer
                    que se dice ser
muy "sensitive."
Ms. Carrerista/proud Feminista
to you. . . .RoAcH.

            "No tengo madre
            ni padre,
            ni un perrito
            que me ladre."
(much less a La Fabulosa . . . bruto!).

El descuento, cucaracho, el descuento.
            ¡Se vale!
Besides,
    you know how
        to do it up
                GOOD!
¿TÚ dirás si destruyemos?

HOME
        is in the arms
cicatrizados/marcados/tatuajados
        con los traques
                    y los callos
Needle-marks
            INJECTED
                (not always by society)
but by one's own kind as well.

Y dice el cuento:
that the Aztec warrior
told an India fair (in Nahua dialect)
"though i must do battle,
adorn my spear with plumage bright
so that THEY know. . .and understand,
i acted out of Love."

Si pudieras volver
        a las jaulas horrorosas
            y avisarle a los demás
¿Qué les dirías?
        ¿qué es ilusión,
            purita diversión
                que no la agarren tan en serio?

¿Qué es puro pedo,
        that folks be living
            instead of giving?

That they be jiving
    a slick conniving,
        the righteous Jeff?
O simplemente,
    that
        the formula
did
  NOT
      work?

Y a según el cuento:
La India then replied
"Should you not return from battle,
it matters not the brilliance
of my Quetzal plumes,
nor the deadly keenness
of your spear. Only that
your cantos (for whatever reasons)
remain to sing of US
in terminology so unique

    CHAIN - ges!

Y los llantos que se oyen
    cada vez
que pasas por la mar
    ¿Qué Pues?

Pero no demore
espejo/imagen/retrato/figura
camarada (salvación y destrucción)
Cucaracho of
        un/FEELINGS.
You/
    i know
        me/you
ev'thang gon' bees aw-right!

Y allí, donde
    El Guerrero cayó
        (refusing to turn back)
dejó grabado/con sangre/en la arena
for future pioneers & foragers,
creators de la Nueva Orden Social
to read n' heed n' carry on:

"Todo Está De Aquéllas!"

RICARDO SÁNCHEZ

— HUECOS Y HUELLAS —

chanting chilenos, llorando
maniobras malditas, sangre
derritiendose sobre calles huecas, huellas
of a sordid past. . .

mundo curtido
by a past washing time/blooded deeds, gentío pobre
perturbed by oppressive weight, no one
wants blame
for having defaulted, duelo
rompiendo lo sagrado de la vida,
death
ravenously propagating unsanity, weep
conciencia de la humanidad, there yet exists
no obra
que cobra
multas
for human desecration, realize
we all are culpable somehow. . .

chanting chilenos, clasping hands
unable to conjoin hope to power
and masters mandate
regimentation
upon empty-bellied masses, non-seeing eyes
need vision toward liberation
and mutable minds need determination
to cast off adumbration. . .

                    allende dead/muertoasesinado,
                    in the ashes of hope
                    where charred ideas are sepulcradas,

chanting chilenos join the legions of the oppressed,
an almost disemboweled people
must plot their way back
to share
in the working of the world. . .

– VIENTO, HISTORY, & DRUM –
POETIC EXPERIMENT IN SOUND

¡ca-túm-ba, ca-túm-ba, tún-tún-pa. . . . . .con/sapos, mis cabrones
cautachones. . . . .ajúa!
y que viva la grasa. . . . .

viento, viento
como caricia,
viento, viento
recuerdo histórico. . .

dejad que tus brisas
bramen mis sueños,
y que las cenizas
y los carbones de mi pasado
suelan rodear
lo más parentético del existir. . .

wind and history, let salient memory and hope burn
their huellas onto
las páginas sucias
of all that has happened;

we seem to only do
that which
is
permissible,
            and even within
            societal abomination
            we cling undaringly. . .
ay,
    ay,
        ay,
PERO QUE DESMADRE, QUE PÉRDIDA TAN HISTÓRICA,

we refuse to listen
to the tamborazos
of our past;

we exist
at the whimsical fringes
of a society unsane;
dressed in caricatured imagery:
            jippified, indiofied, bobbing-greaserfied,
            con gritos refritos
            emulating a nahuatl phantasmagoric fábula
            which never existed,
somos
sombras of all that we could be.
cauterized
into social gelatine, fearful
and unaware
yet groping for a way
to chart out new horizons. . . .

tún-tún-pa, ca-túm-ba, ca-túm-ba, tún-tún-pa,
       yo soy fibra vital,
       the genesis of thought,
       the gestation of feeling,
       the manifestation of being,

       illness cured and well-ness destroyed,
       I am conciencia, nada más y nada menos,
       conscience for a sick/perverted world,
       hope for the moment,
       the fibre of life and the lament you cry
       when death licks its chops while measuring you,
       ill conscience
       locked into your mind and soul,

I shall look deep into my soul, for even consciences have souls, and
recall the past for you; I, also being Chicano, know the anomie of
parenthetical and peripheral existence that you suffer. Like you,
I have also forgotten the indigenous sounds that once held forth
in this our land — yes, before there were nahuatl words, we existed
here indigenously . . . en los pueblos de nuevo méxico, colorado, arizona
tejas, y otras tierras, we sang and laughed and loved and cried out
what it meant to be eso que se llama liberado. . .and the drums of life
cantaban y gritaban un festejo vital amidst montaña y valle, cañón y
peñasco: Libres éramos, gente sencilla, living with woods and
earth, cielo y nube. . .los sonidos eran fuertes y a veces tiernos
como el atole o el chaquehue; crying tamboras son-sonando:

              ca-túm-ba, ca-túm-ba,
                   tún-tún-pa,
              ca-túm-ba, ca-túm-ba,
                   tún-tún-pa,

and I remember,
o' drum of my people,
chicano drum, indígeno drum,
beating out sounds
from montaña y valle
to barrio y campo
universal sound
of creek water merging
into calles y callejones
with furious beat and ritmo,

              ca-túm-ba, ca-túm-ba,
                   tún-tún-pa,
              ca-túm-ba, ca-túm-ba,
                   tún-tún-pa,

recuerdo drum beat
signaling
beginning of life
when america was green
and life abounded hopefully
before machine fire

ate up
grasses and smeared clear water. . .

        ca-túm-ba, ca-túm-ba,
                tún-tún-pa,
        ca-túm-ba, ca-túm-ba,
                tún-tún-pa,

I remember,
o' drum of my people,
time and ritmo
before the coming of white waves
devouring all before them,
I remember
chapulín lived
near coyote
and then nahuatl words
flowed/merged
into tewa/mescalero/chiricahua
     and navajo/comanche spheres of being,
and idioma tras idioma spoke of life and love
and universe being center
of one's self, where ombligo
is power,
yes, then
when time swam languidly
without haste,
then when existential praxis
rode with
mountain trail
into steam,
yes, then in the eye of gods,
goddesses, and temples,
jacales and hogans,
and
     mestizo was a word yet to be invented,

I remember, my people,
the pounding of drum
and the ritmo of the cosmos,

        ca-túm-ba, ca-túm-ba,
                tún-tún-pa,
        ca-túm-ba, ca-túm-ba,
                tún-tún-pa,

and the roar of time
becoming weapon whipping us
onward onto serving,
I remember
he came into our lives
merging his beard with our faces,
and his names were
Spanish steel and Toledo credulity,
fierce and proud, profane and real,

still, he came unto the land,
called it tierra
and it uplifted his tiredness.
as he ululated catalán & morisco laments,
orgulloso y castañoso,
caballero y gachupín,
hombre güero o trigueño,
madrileño, moro, judío, o latín,
bien mesclado
y fregado
ha llegado
a fregar—
              combatiente en la selva,
              jornador por el desierto,
              cobrador entre montañas,
              sembrador con sus hazañas—
he lived, that español lived,
without fences
fiercely proclaiming more than rights,
privileged he felt to be,
his castanets and arabic warbles
convoluted
his involuted mind,
and late at night
he heard the weeping
of marina-cum-guadalupe-cum-la-llorona
to the ritmos of tamboras interspersed
with santa-maría-madre-de-chuy,
it was later, much later, after
mestizo became
a people
merged under the sun,
that shadowy reality
resounded tamborazos

                    ca-ta-tuḿ, ca-ta-túm,
                    ca-túm-ba, ca-ta-túm,
                    ma-ca-la-ca, ca-ta-túm,

and un sol ardiente,
quemante sol desgraciado,
soldered body/mind/soul
of our people,
and cycle of oppression changed,

                    ca-ta-túm, ca-ta-túm,
                    ca-túm-ba, ca-ta-túm,
others came
wantonly to despoil,
              not just conquer,
all that stood before them. . .
ay ay ay,
coyote then was lynched,
along with don quixote,
wantonly assassinated,

even foolishly hated,
and the tierra finally tired
spewed up rotted senses
of all that had been life. . .
tambora, tambora,
        tún-tún-pa,
ca-túm-ba, ca-túm-ba,
        tún-tún-pa,

drum of past
merged with now,
disjointed
amidst taco-bell-buildings
like our raza
striving to gringoize themselves,
disjointed
when hope is dead,
disjointed
whe anti-life salivations matter most,
disjointed
when our peoples feel unable to create,
disjointed
when our humanity does not fight its self-defense,
disjointed
when our universal need to sing and shout and be and act out liberation
ceases to beat and beat within our beings. . .

drum, tambora de la raza,
sabemos y tenemos que saber
que
somos nada más
que un pensamiento
vitalmente
awaiting the fulfillment
of that codex called chichitl
when the people of the sun
arise anew to be
a human providence
reclaiming back the earth;
yes, tambora de la tierra,
bronc beating/alma bleating,
mestizaje shall create
un horizonte humano,
a panoramic realness,
a cosmic human-ness,
and you shall sound again
a majestic/ritmo call
to all that we must be. . .
        ca-túm-ba, ca-túm-ba,
            tún-tún-pa,
        ca-túm-ba, ca-túm-ba,
            tún-tún-pa,

y como conciencia y espíritu,
como chicano y pedazo de la historia,

como ser humano y etapa cultural,
i view today perturbado
because la historia has many peoples and many drums,
and la esclavitud se permite
each time a person bows. . .

ca-ta-túm, ca-túm-ba, CA-TA-TÚM. . . . .

MARCELA TRUJILLO

COLORADO

Con rostro rayado, Colorado,
miras hacia el cielo azul,
loas a Dios por ser un estado,
por tu beldad de montañas, adorado.

Vamos a pasar por vista históricas,
Veamos una alborda de siglo pasado
y una escena de una cadena
de picos níveos en su gran primor. . .
. . .Sacudiendo la aureola, asciende el sol
tiñendo bermejo el vasto firmamento
alumbrando arreboles, salpicadas por rayas
destilan y bañan las cimas nevadas,
enlazando así la tierra con el cielo.
. . .La naturaleza en toda su belleza,
arrodilló el cura que lo presenció
y lo bautizó, "La Sangre de Cristo"

En memoria de ese tiempo antiguo,
El fondo del Río * reluce rojizo,
A la haz lleva un penacho de espuma,
espuma espesa que sopla burbujas
y murmura en luto
cantilenas heróicas
de cortejos viejos
de héroes ignotos
cuyas hazañas pasaron
por el páramo aire
para siempre quedar
desconocidas por nosotros
y olvidadas por cronistas.

Reclama historia la tierra colorada,
Teñida por la sangre derramada
de la raza indígena
          que en español hablada
          y a Jesucristo rezaba.

Mas la tierra carmín recobra en vano
las poblaciones y pueblos que dieron grano
          a la herencia y a la cultura
          del indio y del hispano

Y casi con ironía
el maizal todavía
besa el viento del Norte*
en incauta armonía.

El verde zacate escala los montes,
Matizándose morado
al llegar a lo alto,
donde se ven coronadas
las cumbres nevadas.
que por las nubes giran
y al sol desafían
para probar el poder de Dios.

* Con mayúscula porque se refiere al Río Colorado
* Con mayúscula porque se rifiere al continente de
Norteamérica.

TÚ

Por venir acá
te ví
y en ti ví
mi porvenir

VERDE VERDUGO*

Verde vienes a atormentar la vista
que trastorna la sangre y despierta el cuerpo
    con nostalgia necia
    de recuerdos muertos.
¿Por qué no te quedaste?
Bajo el blanco manto del invierno santo
Bajo el blanco manto del invierno santo
    donde yacen trozos
    de los sueños fuertes.
¿Por qué no te quedaste?
Bajo el blanco manto del invierno santo
Bajo el blanco manto del invierno santo
    Helando los brazos
    que claman por amor
¿Por qué no te quedaste?
Bajo el blanco manto del invierno santo
Bajo el blanco manto del invierno santo
    cubriendo ojos mustios
    que se clavan al sol.
¿Por qué no te quedaste?
Bajo el blanco manto del invierno santo
Bajo el blanco manto del invierno santo
¿Por qué no te quedaste?
        Bajo el blanco manto del invierno·
        Bajo el blanco manto del
            Bajo el blanco
            Bajo el blanco
                Bajo el
                Bajo

*Verde Verdugo means The Green Hangman or Execu-
tioner. The concept here is taken from T.S. Eliot and
Rubén Darío, who have written poems which say that
April or Spring is a cruel time of year for the old person
who can only be nostalgic about a youthful love. There
is sanctuary, however, during the Winter when nature
cannot aid the stirring of the emotions, because the
green landscape is covered with snow.

Recent earth disturbances in Managua
both natural and man made in origin
brought visions in hospital bed of
los güesos de mi Papá glistening in the
earth-split morning—desenterrados
güesos that assist me in whatever is
necessary in the proceso de liberación
Liberación de todos nuestros Pueblos
nuestras vidas—from Mindanao to
Wounded Knee
to the universe

EARTH

Y que me sirvan de flauta y verso
o desenterrados güesos de mi padre
güesos/versos bone of my father
flute mi poema/llanto
into the marrow de esta triste noche
o triste noche americana/
flute the song deep deepen
the danza nuestros tatarabuelos
invocaron al sol/madre tierra
y amor-amor   (suenen flautas)

Y que me sirvan de puñales líricos
padre güesos/versos
that I invoke in the name of
freedom/land/love
                    (disparen flautas)

O bury my songs deep o deep
into the skull of "manifest destiny"
and buckle hat pilgrims
sink deep the image of smallpox
mayflower
and glass bead crucifixes
sink them deep now into whale belly
statue of *their* liberties
dance again hoof of buffalo spirit
not silver not nickel
dance again nuestra danza bronce
of indian continent
y cante "nezahualcóyotl" oraciones
pa' america/indiana
          ("That so proudly we'll hail")
          ("That so proudly we'll hail")

O bury deep deep mis versos
in the cracked walls of distorted
histories
o let the lost güesos of truth
shatter now blood and feather
    silence
              (disparen flautas)

que reporten tambores of the real
"Fomenters of Disturbance"
beat drum of semi-automatic
    wounded
knee murder
gatling burst "From the halls of
Moctezuma
burst hotckiss men "bright stars"/
"bright stripes"
burst hotckiss women/children burst
burst all ye faithful all the way
from Alabama to wounded knee
canta indio/black/asian chicanocide
song
    (same sad genocide song)
o chango o deganawidah
    Madre/padre espíritu of the plains
              (preparen las armas)

O bury my song deep o deep
in the heart of POW's disabled
veterans anywhere color images
of sammy davis kissing dick—tap
    dance
rows of $$ crucifixes (sterling

silver) lining Wall St.
striped tie prophets weep (o let us
weep) by I.T.&T. deity or destruction
of chile
million dollar offerings to our lord
C.I.A.
Chas. Atlas dies buried in the sands
of Iwojima/time by all the 97 yr.
wklings
deep pepsicola mafia offers u can't
refuse in terremoto-torn Managua
and Stalingrad. . .U.P.I. photo
of "looters" being shot by Guardia
Nacional
broken bottles of pepsi en la avenida
roosevelt
pictures of amerikind presidents
inside bottletops
motors roar
earth rumbles
U.S. army bulldozing atlantis/
    managua
the song of quetzal rises from
surfaced bone
helicopters whirl 4pm in the mission
b-52s leave all my poems bomb
Cambodia
zamboanga surface ready to the
    bone. . .
deep deep/deep/deep
(to the bone)

Let us bury together deep
the corporate thoughts of
rebuilding sacrilegious hollywood
shrines
in U.S. images of hotdog/pepsi
mutants
baptize monolithic hughes seaplane
    in
Tiscapa
deep deep in washington red tape
the plan of transomosa pyramid II
deep too o bury I.B.M. plátanos
alongside 38 yr. old song sung
en el nombre del padre deep

the somoza son now the other one
Harvard artifacts stamped "In
God We Trust"
"The Rising Cost of Beef Is An Act
of God"
Quote: Ronnie Reagan mar. 27,
    1973
God-Nixon God-Father God-Damn
Que reporten Tambores now army
bulldozer
sandinos güesos resurrected (Big
    Foot)
güesos/indios güesos/semi-automatic
together bury deep conquistadores
    now
in nicaragua
mindanao
y wounded knee
                    (cante quetzal)

O bury deep mis poemas cargadas
llantos mestizos/Toltecas
de neruda y de cardenal
bury DEEP *charged* con el güeso/
    FLAUTA
de mi papá
güeso/verso güeso/pañal Deep
between the thighs of AYER Y HOY
for the birth of LIBERACIÓN
O DEEP SEED SONG OF MAÑANA
"LIBERACIÓN!!   LIBERACIÓN"
                    (preparen los
                    güesos que
                    cante quetzal)

April 5, 1973
    FBI leading Russell Means
    Away for further Negotiations
    In Handcuffs. . .
    In The Middle of America
    In The Name Of The Law
    STOP!!   Ghost Dance?

PEDRO ORTIZ VÁSQUEZ

CASTLES AND KINGS

cardboard castles
en medio del río
dried up for years
como la gente
tierra real donde crecí
i was king and never knew
que fuera de mis
cardboard castles
habían otros mundos

tierra de mi nacimiento
do you still exist
barren cradle
abandonada rejected
if i return tierra santa
me recibirás
como la madre recibe
a su hijo

cardboard castles (que nombre)
donde crecí
i was king and never knew
que fuera de mis
castillos de cartón
there were other worlds

máscara máscara
faces pintadas
yellow y rojas
negras y brown
blanca today
tomorrow azul
nadie lo sabe
which cara
is true

máscara máscara
pobre man
hombre rich
pregnant mujer
niño aborted
child bautismo
máscara máscara
father y dios

máscara máscara
prisoners de querra
boycott sexual carne
stolen indian tierra
faces cambiando
colores clean
máscara máscara
máscara máscara

diga señor newsman
nuevas de today
muerte suerte
living
fuerte miedo
being
bombers laos
dejan
playground viejas
changing
easter fiesta party
wealthy sano rey

andamos contigo cuauhtemoc
hombre de bronce
and might
herido vencido
mentiras
my lord
andamos sangrando azteca

seguimos luchando hidalgo
morelos zapata
y villa
indian derechos
de vida y tierra
andamos sangrando azteca

struggle together mexicanos
mano en mano
hermanos
indians chicanos
la raza
my lord
andamos sangrando azteca
my lord
andamos sangrando azteca

QUINCE DAYS

quince days
big nuevas
medio día
good noche
war y paz
santo mas
ya lo ve

wounded knee
jaw quebrada
blistered mano
yanqui score
million dollars
santo mas
ya lo ve

new orlenas
party grande
gente mucha
aqua death
easter fiesta
santo mas
ya lo ve

north vietnam
presidente
gente dying
inocente
blood y tierra
santo mas
ya lo ve

aqua gate
false mentira
channel seis
sports arena
limpia sangre
santo mas
ya lo ve

little niña
nueva life
muerte conquered
weeping padres
modern hombre
santo mas
ya lo ve

fifteen días
treinta days
nothing cambia
grande news
war y paz
santo mas
ya lo ve

entender
understand
tiempos good
malo times
yo no sé
santo mas
ya lo ve

PARA PABLO* (PÁJARO WRITER) 1973

freedom flyer pájaro writer
tu luz que brilla solamente
tu mano la apaga
twenty-six years ago pájaro
you came this way
the hunted one
the chased one
de chile a méxico
y todavía el gran casador
del mundo te busca he follows you
and others of your breed
y porque tú eres lo que eres
pájaro writer valiente freedom flyer
tu especie crece en vez de disappearing
y aunque tú ya mueres
sea de enfermedad o de balazos extranjeros
you have opened up our hearts to feeling
to sharing our hopes and our dreams
tú y tus hermanos nos han hecho vigilantes
y guardias de la vida aquí y en tu país
donde caíste pájaro sangrado
y en los mundos donde viajaste
tus obras bien hechas pablo
will continue como pájaros volando
free spirits freedom flyers
con nosotros los pájaro writers
siguiendo la luz que brilla y solamente
nuestra mano la puede apagar

*pablo neruda

TINO VILLANUEVA

CONSIDERANDO EN FRÍO, IMPARCIALMENTE, CÉSAR**

Considerando en frío, imparcialmente, César,
que moriste en París sin aguacero,
un día Viernes Santo de primavera,
un día del cual no puedo ya olvidar. . .

Considerando
que gemebundo lamentabas la angustia
de tu espíritu que por 112 días
encarcelaron en Trujillo,
y otra vez quebrantaron
en un sanguinolento julio,
y que por ende, fe en el hombre
habías tú perdido. . .

Comprendiendo sin esfuerzo
que el hombre de mi Raza todavía suda,
pero ahora grita ¡BASTA!
. . . *from sea to shing sea.* . .

Considerando también
que la familia de Davy Crockett se apoderó de Texas,
y Smokey the Bear de Nuevo México;
que nos pegan todos
sin que nosotros les hagamos nada. . .

Examinando, en fin,
nuestro ánimo y ahínco,
aun después de un largo siglo atroz. . .

Comprendiendo
que Corky, José Angel, Dolores Huerta,
Tijerina, Enriqueta Vásquez, y claro,
tu tocayo de Delano,
más tres aulas llenas de académicos
que ahora nos rescatan para nunca jamás
ser nosotros *criminals of a scholarly society.* . .

Considerando nuestros documentos
y Planes específicos que muestran
que somos una hábil masa inquebrantable. . .

te hago saber, César, que vamos ganando terreno;
son testigos el quinto sol, los días hábiles,
la piel de bronce, el Carnalismo, los surcos,
el grito audaz y el águila negra.

174

Y si pudieras ver al Hombre ahora, César,
te quedarías (estoy seguro)
emocionado. . . Emocionado. . .

**Con los siguientes textos a la mano: "Consideran-
do en frío, imparcialmente", y "Piedra negra sobre una
piedra blanca" de César Vallejo.

VARIATION ON A THEME BY WILLIAM CARLOS WILLIAMS

I have eaten
the *tamales*
that were on
the stove heating

and which
you were probably
having
for dinner

Perdóname
they were *riquísimos*
so juicy
and so steaming hot

NOT KNOWING, IN AZTLÁN

the way they look at you
    the schoolteachers
the way they look at you
    the City Hall clerks
the way they look at you
    the cops
    the airport marshalls
the way they look at you

You don't know if it's something you did
    or something you are

NUESTROS ABUELOS

*Who are the plaintiffs? It is the conquered who
are humbled before the conqueror asking for his
protection, while enjoying what little their mis-
fortune has left them. . . They do not understand
the prevalent language of their native soil. They
are strangers in their own land.***

Nuestros abuelos
in their private suffering
toiled
between the four winds of heaven
& the fifth sun.

Sus espaldas carried ties
for iron-horse companies;
sus coyunturas genuflected
for other similar go-West-young-man
enterprises.

Sus manos se hincharon de años
y de callos y por eso
sus cuerpos,
cansadas cicatrices,
han llegado
hasta la humilde tumba.

**From the eloquent speech delivered on April 26, 1856 by the Honorable
Don Pablo de la Guerra, in opposition of the "law to settle and titles in
California" which was approved by the Legislature in 1856. Excerpt of speech
appeared in *EL GRITO,* Vol. V, No. 1, Fall 1971.

NON-ODE TO THE TEXAS RANGERS

> . . . the Rangers among Mexican Americans have a
> good reputation.

> *Words of Texas Ranger Capt. A. Y. Allee**

> Pasan, si quieren pasar,
> y ocultan en la cabeza
> una vaga astronomía
> de pistolas inconcretas.

> *Romance de la Guardia Civil Española,*
> Federico García Lorca

Day breaks raw
under siege. Time strikes dumb the dawn
down the broad-shouldered Interstate —

> make way
> for the lone-tin-stars spangling the shrouded myth/
> fleet machines
> driven by double-brute barreling
> down/
> through/
> up/
> into post-1848 barrios—ovens of tragedian Valley.

> Again to murder Spanish and the tongue/
> murder incorporated
> into your glance/your long-range aim js clear/
> no questions asked/
> mobile chambers of justice at pointblank
> gunning
> down
> also the mind
> in front of *El Buen Redentor* Baptist Church/
> we have witnesses/
> choir members came chorally screaming:

> *¡Socorro! Tres rinches,* one riot!

We've been told this news before
on this same unpaved crossroads where
bicultural dreams are shattered:

> had just returned from *las piscas*
> this man of the soil— Pancho Anónimo was/is
> his name/gypsy-bronzed/
> caught in the flash of a leaded wind/
> his hands were in his pocket but the
> blast blew loose his stride &
> stunned him still in a pool of splash/
> there's gravel or is it shrapnel in his stare.

Another borderline case but his wounds
are deeper than blood three pints full
soaking & seeding our soil.

***

Without warning
then & there
you leave behind
one Spring day hemorrhaging to death
under metallic-blue sky/high wide sky
gauzed with Andalusian clouds— only your damn bluebonnets
are left intact.

***

I still maintain:

    my scars shall haunt your children/
    Chicano blood shall ransom
    pint
    by
    pint
    the blood shed here/

    or my skin's not brown.

---

* So stated Capt. Alee on the witness stand on the last
day of the U.S. Commission on Civil Rights hearings at San
Antonio, Texas, December 14, 1968. Quote taken from the
San Antonio Sunday Express and News, December 15, 1968.
(The author.)

SYLVIA ZARAGOZA

¿QUÉ MÁS QUIEREN?

Hay mis niños, ¿qué pasa?
¿Por qué están llorando?
¿Por qué están peleando?
¿En qué están gritando?

Hay mamá, falta de saber de las cosas que están pasando.
Estamos llorando por la paz del barrio.
Estamos gritando por la Raza nuestra.

Mis niños, niños grandes.
¿En qué puedo ayudarles?
Yo sé que estoy vieja;
Yo sé que no más hablo español;
Yo sé que es imposible cambiarme, yo sola.

Mamá, no tienes que cambiar total.
Yo sé que has vivido una vida difícil.
Yo sé que fuimos niños de lumbre.
Pero, queremos vivir una vida entre de
estilo mexicano y americano.

Hay mis niños ¿qué pasa?
¿Por qué tienen que vivir una vida Americana?
¿No te parece que vivíamos una vida libre y pacífica?
¿No te parece que fuimos padres buenos?
¿No te parece que toda la gente era buena con nosotros?

Sí, como no, Mamá.
Pero, ahora es diferente.
Tenemos que ayudar a la Raza nuestra;
Tenemos que decir a la Raza que hay gente que
quieren sacarnos afuera de la vida.
Tenemos que educarnos, hablarnos, y ayudarnos
para progresar.
Mis niños buenos, a progresar ¿cómo?
Ya tenemos casa.
Ya tenemos dinero;
Ya tenemos la comida;
¿Qué más quieren?

179

DEATH

I wonder how many
Chicanos are here in
the city

I wonder how many are
afraid

I wonder how much does
it take to see,
how much of life Chicanos
must stake

It isn't a question of
seniority nor
a question of fight

It is a question of ability
to lose less than life

elections

...r "Zeta" Acosta
...van Arellano
...d Gómez
...ando R. Hinojosa S.

OSCAR "ZETA" ACOSTA

SELECTION FROM
THE REVOLT OF THE COCKROACH PEOPLE

It is early one morning when the family of Robert Fernández arrives. The sign outside the basement office only announces *La Voz*, but these strangers come in asking for me. Via the grapevine, they have heard of a lawyer who might help them. Nobody else is around. It is just them and me:

"We gotta have someone to help us, Mr. Brown. The deputies killed my brother."

A hefty woman with solid arms and thick mascara burnt into her skin is talking. She says her name is Lupe. She is the spokesman, the eldest child in a family of nine. The woman beside her is the mother, Juana, an old nurse. Juana is still in shock, sitting quietly, staring at Gilbert's paintings hung on the wall. John, Lupe's husband, sits on her other side. His arms are crossed, bright tattoos over corded muscle. He wears a white T shirt and a blue beanie, the traditional garb of the *vato loco,* the Chicano street freak who lives on a steady diet of pills, dope and wine. He does not move behind his thick mustache. He too sits quietly, as a proper brother-in-law, a cuñado who does not interfere in family business unless asked.

"Why do you say they killed your brother?" I ask.

"¡Porque son marranos!" Juana cries out and then falls back into silence, Aztec designs in black and red meet her glazed eyes.

I ask for the whole story. . . .

Robert was seventeen when the weight of his hundred and eighty pounds snapped the bones and nerves of his fat brown neck. He, too, lived in Tooner Flats, a neighborhood of shacks and clotheslines and dirty back yards. At every other corner, street lights hang high on telephone poles and cast dim yellow glows. Skinny dogs and wormy cats sniff garbage cans in the alleys. Tooner Flats is the area of gangs who spend their last dime on short dogs of T-Bird wine, where the average kid has eight years of school. Everybody there gets some kind of welfare.

You learn about life from the toughest guy in the neighborhood. You smoke your first joint in an alley at the age of ten; you take your first hit of *carga* before you get laid; and you learn how to make your mark on the wall before you learn how to write. Your friends know you to be a *vato loco,* a crazy guy, and they call you *"ese,"* or *"vato,"* or "man." And when you prove you can take it, that you don't cop to nothing even if it means getting your ass whipped by some other gang or the cops, then you are allowed to put your mark, your initial, your sign, your badge, your *placa* on your turf with the name or initial of your gang: White Fence, Cuatro Flats, Barrio Nuevo, The Jokers, The Bachelors, or what have you. You write it big and fancy, scroll-like, cholo print. Grafitti on all the stores, all the garages, everywhere that you control or claim. It's like the pissing of a dog on a post. And underneath your *placa,* you always put C/S, *"Con safos,"* that is: *Up yours if you don't like it, ese!*

There is no school for a *vato loco.* There is no job in sight. His only hope is for a quick score. Reds and Ripple mixed with a bennie, a white and a toke. And

181

when your head is tight, you go down to the hangout and wait for the next score.

On the day he died, Robert had popped reds with wine and then conked out for a few hours. When he awoke he was ready for more. But first he went to Cronie's on Whittier Boulevard, the Chicano Sunset Strip. Every other door is a bar, a pawn shop or a liquor store. Hustlers roam freely across asphalt decorated with vomit and dogshit. If you score in East Los Angeles, you score on the Boulevard. Broads, booze and dope. Cops on every corner make no difference: the fuzz, *la placa, la chota, los marranos, la jura* or just the plain old pig, the eternal enemies of the people. The East LA Sheriff's substation is only three blocks away on Third Street, right alongside the Pomona Freeway. From the Blockhouse, deputies come out in teams of two, "To Serve and Protect!" Always with thirty-six-inch clubs, with walkie-talkies in hand; always with gray helmets, shotguns in the car and .357 Magnums in their holsters.

The *vato loco* has been fighting with the pig since the Anglos stole his land in the last century. He will continue to fight until he is exterminated.

Robert had *his* last fight in January of 1970. He met his sister, Lupe, at Cronie's. She was eating a hamburger. He was dry, he told her. Would she please go to the store across the street and get him a six-pack on credit? No, she'd pay for it. Tomorrow is his birthday so she will help him celebrate it early. Lupe left Robert with friends. They were drinking cokes and listening to the jukebox. Robert liked *mayate* music, the blues. They put in their dimes and sip on cokes, hoping some broad, a *ruka,* would come buy them a hamburger or share a joint with them.

I know Cronie's well. I live two blocks away with the three cousins. I know if you sit on the benches under the canopy long enough, *someone* comes along with *something* for the evening's action. This time the cops brought it.

By the time Lupe returned with a six-pack, two deputies were talking with Robert and his friends. It all began, he told her when she walked up, just because he shouted "Chicano Power!" and raised his fist.

"The cop told me to stay out of it, Mr. Brown. I told him Robert is my brother. But they told me to get away or else they'd arrest me for interfering, you know."

Juana says, "Tell him about the dirty greaser."

"Oh, yes. . . . We know this pig. He's a Chicano. Twice he's arrested Robert," Lupe says.

"Yes, Mr. Brown!" Juana could not restrain herself. "That same man once beat up my boy. He came in one day, about a year ago, and he just pushed into the room where Robert was sleeping. He dragged him out and they held him for three days. . . . They thought he had stolen a car. . . . But the judge threw the case out of court. That pig hated my boy."

Robert had been in jail many times. He'd spent some time at the Youth Authority Camp. But he'd been off smack over a year now. He still dropped a few reds now and then. And yes, he drank wine. But he was clean now. The cops took him in from Cronie's, they said, to check him out. They wanted to see if the marks on his arms were fresh. But anyone could tell they were old.

Lupe appeals to John:

"That's the truth, Brown," the brother-in-law says. "Robert had cleaned up. He even got a job. He was going to start working next week."

"And we were going to have a birthday party for him that Friday," Juana says.

The deputies took Robert and told Lupe not to bother arranging bail. They told her he'd be released within a couple of hours. They thought he might just be drunk, but mainly they wanted to check out his arms. They said for her not to worry.

An hour after he was arrested, Robert called his mother. The cops had changed their minds, he said. They had booked him for Plain Drunk, a misdemeanor. The bail was set at five hundred dollars.

"He told me to call up Maldonado, his bail bondsman. Robert always used him. I could get him out just like that. All I had to do was make a phone call and then go down and sign, you know? The office is just down the street. I didn't even have to put up the house or anything. Mr. Maldonado always just got him out on my word!" the mother cries.

Juana had called the bail bondsman before she received the second call. This time it was a cop. He simply wanted to tell her that Robert was dead. He'd just hung himself. And would she come down and identify the body.

"He was so cold, Mr. Brown. He didn't say he was sorry or anything like that. He just said for me to wait there and he'd send a deputy to pick me up," she says bitterly.

"I went with her," John says. "When we got there I told the man right away that they'd made some mistake. I told him Robert had just called.

"Then they brought in a picture. And I said, *'gracias a Dios,'* I knew him. It wasn't Robert, it was somebody named Sánchez. But that lieutenant said there was no mistake. He said the picture just didn't come out too good.... But Juana told him, 'Well I should know, he's my son.' And I told him Robert wouldn't do a thing like that. He'd never kill himself. He was *católico, Señor Café.* He even used to be an altar boy one time. And he was going to get married, too. He was going to announce it at his party. I talked to Pattie and she told me. She said they were going to get married as soon as he got his first paycheck."

"Pattie is pregnant," Lupe says. "You might as well know, Mr. Brown."

"So what happened after that," I ask.

"We had the funeral and they buried him last week," Juana says.

Lupe says, "We just got the certificate last night. It says he killed himself. Suicide, it says."

"That's a goddamn lie," John says. "Excuse me. . . . But it is."

"How do you think he was killed?"

"I *know*," Lupe says. "At the funeral . . . you tell him, John."

"Yeah, I was there. I saw it."

Doris, another sister, had discovered it. At the funeral, while the others sat and cried, Doris had gone up to get her last look at the body. She bent over the casket to kiss him. Tears from her own eyes landed on the boy's face. She reached over to wipe the wetness from his cheek when she noticed purple spots on the nose. She wiped away the tears and the undertaker's white powder came off his face. It was purple underneath. She called John over and he verified it. They began to look more closely and noticed bruises on the knuckles.

"We told the doctor at the Coroner's Office," John finishes. "But he said not to worry about it. It was natural, he said."

"Anything else?"

"Just what Mr. de Silva told me," the mother says.

"Who's that?"

"Andy de Silva. . . . Don't you know him?"

"You mean . . . *the* Andy de Silva? The man who makes commercials? Chile Charlie?"

"Yeah, that's Mr. de Silva."

I know of him. He is a small-time politico in East LA. A bit actor in grade B movies who owns a bar on The Boulevard. And he considers himself something of a spokesman for the Chicano. He served on Mayor Yorty's Chicano Community Board as a rubber-stamp nigger for the establishment. He and his cronies, the small businessmen and a few hack judges, could always be counted on to the endorse whatever program the Anglo laid out for the Cockroaches. He had been quoted in all the papers during our uprising against the Church. He had agreed with the Cardinal that we were all outside agitators who should be driven out on a rail.

"What did Andy say to you?" I ask.

"Well, I don't even know him. I used to go to his meetings for the old people. Anyway, he called me the next day after Robert died. He said, 'I heard about your boy and I want to help.' That's how he started out. I was so happy to get someone to help I told him to do whatever he could. He said he was very angry and he would investigate the case. He said he would have a talk with the lieutenant and even with the captain if necessary.

"What happened?"

"He called me back the next day. He said he had checked it all out and that the captain had showed him everything, the files and even the cell. He said not to make any trouble. That Robert had hung himself."

"Did he say how he knew about it?"

"Yeah, I asked him that, too," John says.

"He said his nephew was the guy in the cell with Robert."

"His nephew?"

"Yeah, Mickey de Silva . . . He's just a kid like Robert. He was in there for something. . . . Anyway, Andy said his nephew told him that Robert killed himself."

"But we don't believe it," Lupe says fiercely.

"Can you help us, Señor Brown?"

I pick up the phone and dial the office of Thomas Naguchi, the Coroner for the City and County of Los Angeles.

"This is Buffalo Z. Brown. I represent the family of Robert Fernández," I tell Naguchi. "And we want to talk with you about the autopsy. . . . Your doctor listed it as suicide. However, we are convinced that the boy was murdered. We have information unavailable to the pathologist conducting the autopsy. I plan to be in your office this afternoon. I'm going to bring as many people as I can and hold a press conference right outside your door."

"Mr. Brown. Please, calm yourself. I can't interfere with the findings of my staff."

"I'll be there around one."

I hang up and tell the family to go home, call all their friends and relatives and have them meet me in the basement of the Hall of Justice. They thank me and leave. I then call the press and announce the demonstration and press conference for that afternoon. I know my man. And since Naguchi can read the newspapers, my man knows me. The afternoon will be pure ham.

Naguchi has been in the news quite a bit. He was charged with misconduct in office by members of his own staff. They accused him of erratic behavior and incompetence. They said he took pills, that he was strung out, and hinted that perhaps he was a bit nuts. After the assassination of Robert Kennedy he allegedly said he was glad Kennedy was killed in his jurisdiction. He was a publicity hound, they contended. He was removed from his position of County Coroner. He hired a smart lawyer and challenged it. The Civil Service hearings were televised. The white liberals and his own Japanese friends came to his defense. He was completely exonerated. At least he got his job back.

A month prior to the death of Fernández, both the new City Chief of Police, Judd Davis and the sheriff of LA County, Peter Peaches, announced they would no longer request Coroner's Inquests. The publicity served no useful purpose, the lawmen stated. Since the only time the Coroner held an inquest was when a law enforcement officer was involved in the death of a minority person, they contended that the inquest merely served to inflame the community. Naguchi made no comment at the time of this statement, although his two main clients were emasculating his office.

When we arrive at the Hall of Justice, the press is waiting. The corridor is lined with Fernández' friends and relatives. The television cameras turn on their hot lights as I walk in with my red, white and green briefcase, the immediate family at my side.

"Are you making any accusations, Mr. Brown?" a CBS man asks.

"Not now, gentlemen. I plan to have a conference with Dr. Naguchi first. Then I'll speak to you."

I hurried into the Coroner's Office. The people shout "Viva Brown!" as I close the door. The blonde secretary tells me Naguchi is waiting for me. She opens the door to his office and ushers me in.

"Ah, Mr. Brown, I am so happy to make your acquaintance."

He is a skinny Jap with bug eyes. He wears a yellow sport coat and a red tie and sits at a huge mahogany desk with a green dragon paperweight. The office has black leather couches and soft chairs, a thick shag rug and inscrutable art work. It seems a nice quiet place. He points me to a fine chair.

"Now Mr. Brown, I'd like you to read this." He hands me a typed sheet of white paper.

I smile and read the paper:

> *The Coroner's Office announced today that it will hold a second autopsy and an inquest into the death of Robert Fernández at the request of the family through their attorney, Mr. Buffalo Z. Brown. It will be the first time in the history of the office that an inquest is being held at the request of the family.*
>
>   Thomas A. Naguchi
>   County Coroner

I looked into the beady eyes of Mr. Moto. He is everything his men say. "I've been wanting to meet you, Sir," I say.

"And I've heard about you, Mr. Brown. You get a lot of coverage in your work."

"I guess the press is interested in my cases."

"Would you be agreeable to holding a joint press conference?"

"Sir, I would be honored. . . . But one thing . . . If we have another autopsy, the body will have to be, uh. . . ." I am coy.

"Exhumed . . . We will take care of that, don't you worry."

"And who will perform the autopsy?"

"I assume the family will want their own pathologist."

I looked down at his spit-shined loafers. I shake my head and sigh.

"I just don't know. . . . The family is extremely poor."

"I understand, sir. I offer my staff, sir."

"Dr. Naguchi . . . would it be too much to ask you, *personally,* to examine the boy's body? I know you are very busy. . . ." It is my trump card.

"I would be honored. But to avoid any . . . problems, why don't I call up the Board of Pathologists for the county. I will request a panel. Yes, a panel of seven expert pathologists. It will be as careful and as detailed an autopsy as we had for Senator Kennedy. And it won't cost the family anything . . . I have that power."

I stand up and, walking over to him, I shake his hand.

"Dr. Naguchi, I'll be glad to let you do all the talking to the press."

"Oh no, Mr. Brown, it is your press conference."

He calls his secretary and tells her to bring in the boys. When they arrive with their pads and cameras, he greets them all by their first names. He is better than Cecil B. DeMille. His secretary has passed out copies of his statement. He tells them all where to sit and knows how many lumps of sugar they want in their coffee. Then he introduces me to them and stands by while I speak.

"Gentlemen, I'll make it short. . . . We have reason to believe that Robert

Fernández died at the hands of another. The autopsy was inconclusive and we have since found some new evidence that was not available to Dr. Naguchi's staff. . . . The Doctor has graciously consented to exhume the body and hold a full inquest before a jury. On behalf of the family and those of us in East LA who are interested in justice, I would like to thank Dr. Naguchi."

After the press leaves, I reassure the family and all the arrangements are nailed down.

The following Tuesday, I again enter the Hall of Justice. Above me are Sirhan Sirhan, the mysterious Arab who shot Kennedy, and Charles Manson, the acid fascist. Both await their doom. I am told to go straight down the corridor, turn right and the first door to my left is where I'll find Dr. Naguchi and his seven expert pathologists. The light is dim, the hard floors waxed. Another government building with gray walls, the smell of alcohol in night air.

I open a swinging yellow door and immediately find myself inside a large dark room full of hospital carts. Naked bodies are stretched out on them. Bodies of red and purple meat; bodies of men with white skin gone yellow; bodies of black men with blood over torn faces. This one has an arm missing. The stub is tied off with plastic string. The red-headed woman with full breasts? Someone has ripped the right ear from her head. The genitals of that spade are packed with towels. Look at it! Listen! The blood is still gurgling. There, an old wino, his legs crushed, mangled, gone to mere meat. And there, young boys die too. And there, a once-beautiful chick, look at her. How many boys tried to get between those legs, now dangling pools of red-black blood?

Don't turn away from it, goddamnit! Don't be afraid of bare-ass naked death. Hold your head up, open your eyes, don't be embarrassed, boy! I walk forward, I hold my breath. My head is buzzing, my neck is taut, my hands are wet and I cannot look away from the dead cunts, the frizzled balls, the lumps of tit, the fat asses of white meat.

I have turned the wrong way. Backtracking, I find the room with Dr. Naguchi and the experts.

The doctors wear white smocks. They smoke pipes. Relaxed men at their trade. They smile and shake my hand. In front of us, the casket is on a cart with small wheels. On a clean table we have scales and bottles of clear liquid. There are razor-sharp tools, tweezers, clips, scissors, hacksaws, needles and plenty of yellow gloves. The white fluorescent light shines down upon us. It reminds me of the title of my first book: *My Cart for My Casket.*

"Shall we begin, gentlemen?" Dr. Naguchi asks the experts.

The orderly, a giant sporting an immense mustache, takes a card and a plastic seal from the casket. He booms it out to a gray-haired fag with sweet eyes who sits in a corner and records on a shorthand machine.

"We shall now open the casket, Coroner's number 19444889, Robert Fernández, deceased."

We all gather close to get the first look.

The body is intact, dressed in fine linen. Clearly, Robert was a bull of a man. He had big arms and legs and a thick neck now gone purple. Two experts lift the body and roll it on the operating table. It holds a rosary in the hands. The orderly removes the rosary, the black suit, the white shirt, the underwear and brown shoes. The chest has been sewn together. Now the orderly unstitches it. Snip, snip, snip. Holding open the rib cage, he carefully pulls out plastic packages from inside the chest cavity. I hold my breath.

"Intestines." The meat is weighed out.

"Heart . . . Liver. . . ."

A Chinese expert is making notations of everything. So is the fruity stenographer.

There is no blood, no gory scene. All is cold and dry. Sand and sawdust spill to the table.

"Is this your first autopsy?" a doctor with a Sherlock Holmes pipe asks me. I nod.

"You're doing pretty good."

"He'll get used to it," another one says brightly.

When the organs are all weighed out, Dr. Naguchi says, "Now, gentlemen, where do you want to begin?"

Sherlock Holmes asks, "Are we looking for anything special?"

"Treat this as an ordinary autopsy, Dr. Rubenstein. Just the routine," says Naguchi.

"Circumstances of death?"

"Well, uh . . . Mr. Brown?"

"He was found with something around his neck."

"Photographs at the scene?"

"No sir," a tall man from the Sheriff's Department says.

"Self-strangulation? . . . or . . ." Rubenstein lets it hang.

"That's the *issue*," I say. "The body was found in a jail cell. The Sheriff claims it was suicide. . . . We, however, believe otherwise."

"I see."

"We have reason to believe that the boy was murdered," I say.

"Nonsense," the man from the Sheriff's Department says.

"Now, gentlemen, please. . . ." Naguchi oils in.

Dr. Rubenstein is obviously the big cheese. He comes up to me and says, "You think there was a struggle before death?"

"It's very possible."

He ponders this and then announces: "Gentlemen, we will have to dissect wherever hematoma appears."

"What's that?" I ask.

"Bruises."

I look at the body closely. I noticed purple spots on the face, the arms, the hands, the chest, the neck and the legs. Everywhere. I point to the face. "Could *that* be a bruise?"

"There's no way to tell without microscopic observation," Rubenstein answers.

"You can't tell from the *color?*"

"No . . . The body is going through decomposition and discoloration . . . purple spots . . . is normal. You find it on all dead bodies."

"Are you saying we have to cut out all those spots?"

"That's the only way to satisfy your . . . yes."

"Well, Mr. Brown?" says Naguchi. "Where do you want us to begin?"

I look around at the men in the room. Seven experts, Dr. Naguchi and a Chinese doctor from his staff, the orderly and the man from the Sheriff's . . . they want *me*, a Chicano lawyer, to tell them where to begin. They want *me* to direct them. It is too fantastic to take seriously.

"How about this? Can you look there?" I point to the left cheek.

Without a word, the Chinese doctor picks up a scalpel and slices off an inch of meat. . . . He picks it up with the tweezers and plunks it into a jar of clear liquid.

"And now, Mr. Brown?" says Naguchi.

I cannot believe what is happening. I lean over the body and look at the ears. Can they get a notch from the left one?

Slit-slit-slice blut! . . . into a jar.

"Uh, Dr. Rubenstein? . . . Are you *sure* there's no other way?"

He nods slowly. "Usually, we only try a couple of places . . . It depends on the family." He hesitates, then says, "Is the case that important?"

"Would you please take a sample from the knuckles . . . here?"

No trouble at all, my man. Siss-sizz-sem . . . blut, into another jar.

The orderly is precisely labeling each jar. Dr. Naguchi is walking around like a Hollywood mogul. He is smiling. Everything is going without a hitch. He touches my shoulder.

"Just tell us what you want, Mr. Brown. . . . We're at your service."

"Would you please try the legs? . . . Those big splotches on the left."

"How about the chin?"

"Here, on the left side of the face."

"What's this on the neck?"

"Try this little spot here."

"We're this far into it. . . . Get a piece from the stomach there."

Cut here. Slice there. Here. There. Cut, cut, cut! Slice, slice slice! And into a jar. Soon we have a whole row of jars with little pieces of meat.

Hrumph! Yes, men? Now we'll open up the head. See where it's stitched? They opened it at the first autopsy. See the sand fall out from the brain area? Yes, keeps the body together for a funeral. No blood in here, boy. Just sand. We don't want a mess. See that little package? That, my lad, is the brain. I mean, it was the brain. Well, actually, it *still* is the brain . . . it just isn't working right now.

Yes, yes! Now we pull back the head. Scalp-um this lad here. Whoops, the hair, the full head of hair, now it lays back, folded back like a halloween mask so we can look *into* the head . . . inside, where the stuffings for the . . . Jesus H. Christ, look at those little purple blotches. . . . You can tell a lot from that, but you got to cut it out. . . . Then cut the fucking thing out, you motherfucker! This ain't Robert no more. It's just a . . . no, not a body . . . body is a whole . . . this is a joke. . . . Cut that piece there, doctor. *Please!*

Uh oh! Now we get really serious. If he died of strangulation . . . We'll have to pull out the . . . uh, neck bone.

Go right ahead, *sir!* Pull out that goddamn gizzard.

Uh, we have to. . .take the face off first.

Well, Jesus Christ, go ahead!

Slit. One slice. Slit. Up goes the chin. Lift it right up over the face . . . the face? The face goes up over the head. The head? The head is the face. Huh? *There is no face!*

What do you mean?

The face is hanging down the back of the head. The face is a mask. The mouth is where the brain . . . The nose is at the back of the neck. The hair is the ears. The brown nose is hanging where the neck. . . . Get your goddamn hand out of there.

My hand?

That is the doctor's hand. It is inside the fucking face.

I mean the head.

His hand is inside. It is pulling at something. What did he find in there. What is it?

He's trying to pull out the . . . if we put it under a microscope, we'll be able to make some strong findings. It's up to you. . . .

Slice, slice, slice . . . No dice.

"Give me the saw, please."

Saw, saw, saw, saw, saw . . . No luck.

"Give me the chisel and hammer, please."

The goddamn face is gone; the head is wide open; no mouth, nose, eyes. They are hanging down the back of the neck. God! With hammer and chisel in hand, the Chinese doctor goes to town. Chomp, chomp, chomp . . . Hack, hack, chuck, chuck, chud, chomp!

Ah! Got it!

Out it comes. Long, gizzard-looking. Twelve inches of red muscle and nerve dripping sawdust. Yes, we'll dissect this old buzzard, too.

How about those ribs? You want some bar-b-que ribs, mister?

Sure, *ese*. Cut those fucking ribs up. Chomp 'em up right now!

"How about the arms? Is there any question of needle marks?"

Yes, they'll claim he was geezing. Cut that arm there. Put it under your machine and tell me later what I want to hear. Tell me they were *old* tracks, you sonofabitch . . . And try the other one.

Why not? The body is no more.

Should we try the dick?

What for? What can you find in a peter?

Maybe he was raped for Christ's sake. Or maybe he raped someone. How should I know? I just work here.

I see the tattoo on his right arm . . . God Almighty! A red heart with blue arrows of love and the word "Mother." And I see the little black cross between the thumb and the trigger finger. A regular *vato loco*. A real *pachuco, ese*.

And when it is done, there is no more Robert. Oh, sure, they put the head back in place. They sew it up as best they can. But there is no part of the body that I have not ordered chopped. I, who am so good and deserving of love. Yes, me, the big *chingón!* I, Mr. Buffalo Z. Brown. Me, I ordered those white men to cut up the brown body of that Chicano boy, just another expendable Cockroach.

Forgive me, Robert, for the sake of the living brown. Forgive me, and forgive me and forgive me. I am no worse off than you. For the rest of my born days, I will suffer the knowledge of your death and your second death and your ashes to my ashes, your dust to my dust . . . Goodbye, *ese*. Viva la Raza!

ESTEVAN ARELLANO

INOCENCIO

"también de gusto se llora como de dolor se canta"
Pasando la noche en el gallinero—primero lo fregó el penco con la polla, luego no desplumar sus barbas de alambre rodillas para atrás; el muelas de gallo de Inocencio dice que cuando no es una cosa son dos o tres. No hacía mucho que había trampado la oreja mocha de elefante cuando pegó el vislumbre de una luz en la pared de su cuartito. Como estaba más tronado que el deasques, Inocencio pensaba que estaba mirando visiones. Reclama el diantres que a veces se imagina comiendo víboras, mascando alacranes y escupiendo lagartijos. Medio levantaba el hueja pelada la cabeza y se limpiaba las lagañas, después se hacía bola en sus cobijas negras de roña, luego se tapaba la jicarita (cuando lo ven le dicen, "la jicarita está blanquiando," indicando que ya se está haciendo canoso) con su almohada parda del sebo de la caspuda. Así chacualeaba en el colchón y se revolcaba, pensando que era pesadilla lo que tenía cuando se oyó un chiflido de automóvil. Al instante se le quitó lo encamorrado y se le vino a la mente algún desvelado despidiéndose.

—Creo que la Comadre Sebastiana le anda moviendo los huesos a algún pariente—dijo él, con aquel miedo bárbaro.

Frunciendo el cerco, entre los dientes hablaba Inocencio, enchinándosele el cuerpo al pensar de la igualadora. Así se jalaba su piochita, ralitamente sembrada en su mentón; sin hallar que hacer, siempre con la maldita tentación del ruido. Y como andaba tecolano, con todos los alambres trocados, hasta más apretaba el *daime*.

Al fin tiró las cobijas al suelo y reflejó el despertador: eran las cinco de la mañana en uno de los relojes. Tiene cuatro. Todos puestos para su convenencia, el sospechoso de Inocencio Uramios Trujillo. Para acabarla de fregar, él apenas había llegado a las tres de la madrugada de sacar el gallo, repartir el quelite, y de:

—Aprender del mundo lo que es un platito de hambre y un saborcito de frío, porque los dientes que se me empiezan a caer no son de viejo, sino de las mordidas que le ha pega'o al mundo y los que me quedan sueltos me sirven de campanas pa' que el pueblo 'onde llegue sepan que llegó el padre de más de cuatro.

Tras y tras predica el falteado de Inocencio nomás se toma su medicina, sea a golpes por la regadera o un humito por las narices. Y eso es con frecuencia, siendo que el médico le recomendó que tomara muchos líquidos, además de sus yerbitas—bueno, como marrubio, asafrán, y un escante de marijuana para los rumos y lo nervioso—para cualquier enfermedad. Suerte que él sólo sufre de un mal: una cruda, pero para que les cuento, como platica que en todo su maldita vida huérfana nomás una peda se ha puesto. Lo ven cargado de liebres y todavía preguntan que si es cazador. Cuando abrió su primer botella a la edad de once primaveras, tiró el tapón para el otro lado de la acequia y hasta el día no ha vuelto a cerrar los ojos sobrio. Entonces si no vale un cero a la izquierda, está como un cacahuate: nomás para comer sirve, como dice el Paisa. Por lo menos el Chango—su sobrenombre entre sus camaradas—se para el cuello percudido de sudor por solo haberse puesto una peda cuando anda en compañía de sus socios.

Le gusta cargarse los elotes. También nunca ha vuelto a ver el sol, porque no se la quita por no ponerse otra, como dice la palomía. Su amigo, el *Pósol,* cuando se quejaba de su aflicción, muy agüitado sentadito cortándose las uñas en una tarima verde, él y su alma en el *motel de los viudos,* el nombre que la plebe le puso a su casa donde vivía desde que enviudó y se fue al jaral, decía: — ¡Ay Dios, si en la peda te ofendo en la cruda me sales debiendo!

Pero para acabarla de chingar, el descarado de Inocencio antes de dirigirse a los de las biblias bajo el sobaco (ustedes saben, los que comen misas y cagan diablos), les dice a sus amigos: —No se dejen curar de médico enfermo— luego les busca las corbas, a la brava cayéndoles: —¿Qué no traen algo pa' poner los tamborcitos de la cabeza a jalar? Sabiendo bien que no son de los que acarrean ronchas escondidas en la suela, pero, si bien sabe que algo le vido el Padre al agua y por eso la bendició.

Perdiendo sueño por andar en la movida: buscando rucas y gallinas; para cuando llegó al chante ya entró todo baliado. La noche entera tuvo la suerte de la culebra: muy arrastrada. El refrancito nos recuerda que el que nace para barrigón aunque lo fajen de chico. Todo lo que sacó esa noche fue el cuello lleno de corucos, las manos rasguñadas y el saco de guangoche vacío, y como no agarró polla, el pobre sufrió. Pobrecito, siempre al más calvo le arrastra el pelo.

Tiene tantas primaveras Inocencio entre los animales, que cuando regresó de la cuacha platica que hablaba en borrega (y andaba como carnero). Y siendo que por los últimos años no ha dejado gallinero sin meter la manopla, ya entiende lo que dicen las gallinas cuando cantan. En las mañanas, a según su tocayo, caracaquean las pobres gallinas: —*Tanto poner y descalzas.* Alea el gallo, la cresta sangrando, y les responde: —Pus, pus por tu querer. No teniendo más remedio, contesta gallina: —Pus, pus, pus por eso. Las pobres gallinas tienen razón de no alcanzarse de tanto poner y descalzas mientras tengan a Inocencio, porque él esculca todos los nidos para poder comprar su inguento. En todas las montañas norteñas no hay uno como él para la garza; así se conocen los taloniadores de gallina entre sí mismos.

POR FIN SE AMARRÓ él los tanates y se asomó por la ventanita a ver qué miraban sus ojos de gavilán. Afuera las luces de una troca pegaban en la azotea, haciendo que las botellas de Pájaro, que le sirven de techo al santuario de Inocencio, relumbraran como prendas. Como vive atrás de la estafeta en un cuartito que anteriormente era la *Cantina de los plomos,* todavía la rechola vieja se junta a pistiar; y como punto de referencia, a todos les pregunta, aunque vivan en el quinto patio: —Yo sé 'onde viven, allá junto a la estafeta a la mano derecha en una casa blanca. Y no asociándose mucho con el chapusero y trampozo (a veces, hasta ladeado es) del inocentón de Inocencio, sólo los otoños para traer leña, se les hizo curiosa la chosa del peón de todos cuando miraron la azotea de vidrio. La gente del "cuanto hay" eran muy sabios cuando decían que al nopal sólo lo van a ver cuando tiene tuna.

Ellos sólo acarrean leña para el fogón de tierra y echarse el caldo encima (dicen: los Martínez sí son hombres, *nojotros* no nos rajamos ¿qué no, primo? usté digales), teniendo gas en lo demás de su casita de cartón moderna. Estos están con tamaña lonja de cuentas en el espinazo ni la toga que hacen, se les hace que sus pedos no jieden, o que nomás sus enchiladas tienen queso—que nunca se habían fijado del adornamento simple y real en la casa de Inocencio. En todo lo que se fijan es en el pretil cayéndose y luego lo vacilan de huevón. Pero Indocencio sabe mejor: —No hay pena más grande la de trabajar—dice.

—¿Qué será eso que relumbra en la 'zotea?
—¡Quién sabe! Parecen jarros, ¡Quién sabe que diablos tendrá este bárbaro! Cuando salga le preguntamos.
En eso rechinó la puerta de su jacal, hecha toda pal quince, al trochi mochi,

de unos orillos que trujo de la maquinita de rajar del *Llano de la Yegua*. Como tiene más suerte que sentido, ya tiene varios años de servicio la puerta que hizo él y el difunto Garañón para atajar el sol y la nieve y milagrosamente está parada por los rezos de los santos y unos clavos mohosos y doblados. Por Dios santito, como dice el Verdadero, le sirve siquiera para repechar el agua. Es tan bárbaro Inocencio que a veces anda tan pedo, que por no salir por palitos para hacer lumbre, le roe la cáscara a los orillos de la puerta. Y lo hace con tanto cuidado, que parece más bien que una nutria—con mucha curia—le entró a la puerta.

Ya salió el hijo de los apretados infiernos haciendo una sombra espantosa, abrochándose su camisa. Salió como se acostó, bastante abrigado; (traiba puesto una camisa azúl sobre una blanca, luego una suera y su buena corbata de gato y arriba de todo su jorongo que le pasó su camarada serumato—que quiere ser manito—del Barrio del Coruco). Y para acabarla de remachar es chango. Todo lo traiba cargado en el hombro, y venía todavía poniéndose los botones y con el chisperío parado de punta, todas desburujadas. Y su cara de indio, de quijadas de vaca, rasguñada por las curvias de la vida.

—¿Qué pasa, qué chinga'os quieren? ¿Qué no pueden ver ojos en otra cara y dejar durmir a uno? Suerte que no recordaron a mi vieja Soleda, porque mi gordita amor sin dientes en el invierno me calienta y en verano me hace sombra, porque antonces quien sabe como les hubiera ido, chivos.

La vieja que tiene ahora quizás la tiene escondida porque nadie la conoce siendo que la primera se la robó su primo—dice el despegado que los que eran sus hijos ahora son sus primos, y se cura—la segunda se le murió de hambre y la tercera se le heló de frío, y ésta quién sabe que trabajos no pasará, si ni leña le tiene.

—Nos despenas *Inny*, aquí. . .a ver si quieres ir a la leña con *nojotros*. Te pagamos unos dos pesos. Que barbaridá, yo no sabía que tenías vieja.

—Chuuuu, como dijía aquél—y se puso Inocencio sus dedos gretudos sobre sus labios partidos de tanto vino—recuerdan a mi vieja y verán como les va a ustedes patas rajadas, colas negras.

—A que *Inny*, ¿Al fin te *jallates* una nalgona pa' no estar solo—o escariota?

Cabrones, ¿qué se les hace que soy huérfano? ¡Chales! Hazte pa' ya, seguro que sí voy; pero voy pa' que no se hele la prima y el angelito que les mandó mi tatita Dios. Les habló bravo Inocencio, pero siempre ·con su risa carrillenta, enseñando sus colmillotes y con la vachita de la noche antes pegada en su jetota, luego abrió la puerta y se subió con los paisanos en la troca.

UNO DE ELLOS trabaja en el Capitolio pegando estampillas-(todos los Inocencios y Pedro Babas dicen que de tanta estampa que ha *lambido* ya tiene la lengua como trapo y por eso es tan tartamudo)—y el otro tiene varios siglos jalando en el Arbol, pisando el mismo maldito botón cuarenta y ocho horas al día (el pobre obliga'o de hacer su diligencia, dice mana Chica.) Y cuando no están mirando un juego de pelota en la televisión corren la garra de políticos, cabresteándolos como caballos viejos. Nomás por poner un pariente en el programa del PEDO, CABADOR, o algotra miseria del gobierno; de barrendero en las escuelas, que les hagan un caminito o les pongan un caño.

Inocencio como no tiene re ni roque y ni quien lo mande, pues les da mucha batería. —Dice el dicho que el pobre aunque madrugue llega tarde. . .pero quien deja sus negocios por los ajenos no tiene juicio—les dijo el terco de Inocencio una vez en junta abierta—como sabe, hablando alrevez—cuando se paró un vecino a quererles vender gato por liebre. Estaba aferrado el Ernie—el arriero de la troca (el vecino)—que siguieran adelante con el propuesto del gobierno (y también a las escondidas *isque* anda diciendo que le vendan sus tierras a los hippies porque son buena gente—durmidos pueda. A que mi gente tan—para que les cuento— al cabo no es más que un experimento pa' traerles casitas a los pobres.

DAVID GÓMEZ

SELECTION FROM *SOMOS CHICANOS*

CHICANOS ARE BUILDING a new nation, Aztlán, where we and our children can be free. The struggle for liberation. . .has produced several important breakthroughs. We have confronted our oppressors again and again, making unyielding institutions respond to our demands for justice, human decency, and respect. These gains represent only a small beginning. In the days ahead, every Chicano will be needed to commit himself — to respond to the call of his blood — by being part of the Chicano movement.

Aztlán will be our own independent, free nation where we will no longer be the colonized, exploited, and abused people we have been for generations. This nation is not a myth or dream but an imminent reality whose foundations are being laid at this moment.* Chicanos want change not only for their children and the future generation, as Ricardo Chávez-Ortiz has eloquently pleaded, we also want change for ourselves — *now.*

White liberals tell us that we can't expect change overnight because deep-rooted problems which are centuries old can only be solved over the long course of years of patient effort. Work within the system, they tell us, so you can make changes from within. While most of us are committed to the long and painstaking process of making social change, we also want to see important changes made right now, overnight, and we know it can be done. The liberals forget that the Spanish *conquistadores* in 1521 toppled and destroyed the Aztec empire and enslaved our people. That was done in three years, which is overnight! The U.S. Army and the American government of occupation in 1848 overturned our social institutions and economic structures and left us politically impotent. That happened not over the course of fifty or one hundred years; it happened overnight!

Our people obviously do not have the military might of fire power to make changes in the same way that the Spaniards and Anglo Americans did. But we have an even greater weapon available to us. Sheer numbers! We are strong because there are so many of us and because *la unión hace la fuerza* (there's power through unity). And we are not alone as we prepare to make changes for ourselves and our families. We are conscious of being part of a bronze continent, an entire continent of similarly oppressed and alienated *raza.* If the Chicano movement continues to develop and our people continue stepping forward to make their demands known, backing them up by physical presence, Aztlán will become a reality overnight.

Some areas where Aztlán is being built:

Economic Development. This is a basic priority. We need more and better jobs, on-the-job training in important skills, adequate salaries, and good working conditions, especially for *Mexicanos* who are not yet citizens and do not speak English. Their vulnerability has made them easily exploitable by unscrupulous employers. Economic control of our communities must also once again reside within the people. What Chicanos are demanding here is not that brown-skinned exploiters replace the white ones that now plague poor people in the *barrios.* We are demanding nothing less than a completely new order, and the advent of a

193

Chicano economics. "They say economics is pure," says Steve Sanora, a Chicano student at California State College, Los Angeles. "Sure, there are certain things about supply and demand, but it becomes Chicano economics when you take into account the social factor. Chicano economics would be supply and demand determined by our social ethic; it's not a monetary profit, it's a social profit we're looking for." That social profit is the equitable distribution of wealth among our people.

Social Equality. The movement has restored ethnic, racial, and cultural pride for millions of us who were brainwashed in Anglo-white schools. Demeaning caricatures of Chicanos as dumb, sinister, lazy, dirty, and so on, have been forced off the advertising market, but the white man's image of us will probably not change until we have won full economic, social and ethnic-racial equality.

The Women's Liberation Movement has contributed many good ideas to Chicana women which they have been able to use in educating the Chicano man. Many Chicanos, of course, still have not yet learned that their women are not merely housekeepers, babysitters, and sex-objects, but *compañeras* (companions and co-equal partners). This is crucial to the movement because as one Chicana told me, *"El movimiento sin mujeres no se gana como el movimiento sin hombres no se gana!"* (without women the movement will not succeed just as the movement without men will not succeed). In the revolution of 1910 in México the *Adelitas* (Mexican women soldiers) fought side by side with their men; without them the war would not have been won. Chicanos have to understand that we are fighting a war now and we need our women alongside us. And those Chicanas who must tend their children at home have an equally important role, because they must educate our children as revolutionaries.

"In no way do I consider the Chicano man my enemy," says Amalia Uribe, a 22-year-old Chicana from Coachella who has worked for César Chávez as a strike leader and is now a labor organizer for the *Hermandad General de Trabajadores* in Los Angeles. "We must be a family, all of us together, for the movement. Where there are differences, we have to educate the man. But in no way do I consider him my foe. I believe that he is another victim of the capitalist system, just as I am. There is no separate movement for women's rights just as there is no separate one for the men. There is only one movement and that is for all our *raza.*"

Political Representation. "Racism is at the root cause of the Chicano's political nonrepresentation," says Hermán Sillas of the California State Advisory Committee to the U.S. Civil Rights Commission. "And this is true on every level of government: municipal, county, state, and federal." This accounts for there being no Chicano mayor for any big city in the Southwest; no state governor; no city councilman in Los Angeles (in proportion to our numbers we should have three out of fifteen), this nation's most populous Chicano city. There are only four Chicano members of the U.S. Congress and only one Chicano in the U.S. Senate. The Man has cheated us out of political power by a variety of means: gerrymandering of our districts; discriminatory language, literacy, and residency requirements; threat of deportations and violence if we became politically active, et cetera.

La Raza Unida Party (LRUP). This third party movement among Chicanos began as opposition to the racist politics of both major political parties. On the local level, especially in the *barrios* and *colonias,* LRUP is an effective political reality. Crystal City, Texas, was the scene of José Angel Gutiérrez's first organizational efforts for LRUP and showed what could be done when Chicanos were organized as a voting bloc; they captured nearly all of the elective offices formerly held by Democrats. In other areas where Chicanos are not a majority, they can still be organized within LRUP as a crucial swing vote, as was done recently in the race for Los Angeles' 48th assemblyman's seat, where LRUP candidate Raúl Ruiz ran as an independent and demonstrated to the Democratic Party that without *raza* support they couldn't win elections. The LRUP vote ensured the defeat of the Democratic candidate in an assembly district that had always been hardcore Democratic; a Republican was elected to office for the first time in the history of that district. In this way, we are winning the respect of the Republicans and teaching the Democrats that we no longer can be taken for granted as their hip-pocket vote.

The Church and La Raza. Chicanos have forced the Catholic Church to make a few token changes within the institution, but it continues to misuse its power, money and political influence (despite denials of being political, any human institution that owns stock in Bank of America, General Motors, et cetera is political!). What is worse, the Church has once again forfeited its moral leadership within our communities by failing to be on the side of the poor in their struggle for self-determination.

I now have no official status or position within the institutional Church, but Chicanos still call on me to celebrate Mass for them, which I am happy to do. Church officials would frown on this, but even the most conservative church-men recognize the validity of my ordination. Moreover, according to the theology most priests learn, there are sacred functions (like baptisms, marriages, Mass, et cetera) which laymen and "defrocked" priests can and should perform in emergency situations when there are no priests available. Most Chicanos believe that as Catholics they are in an emergency situation, because the Church has ceased ministering to their unique cultural and religious needs. In that sense, Anglo priests who do not understand our people are not "available" even though many imposing churches and rectories have been built within the *barrios*. An underground Church for Chicanos is thus slowly coming into existence. This may be the beginnings of our Chicano Catholic Church.

Education. The most important area for development as we build Aztlán is the schools. As we have seen, the schools have acted as the single most divisive force within our communities by teaching us formally and by example that who and what we are in inferior and inadequate. The schools have prevented us from truly knowing ourselves, our history, our accomplishments.

Colleges and universities have also done a great disservice to our people by deceiving people into thinking their programs for "minority groups" were actually helping *raza* advance within society. These institutions have established "minority admissions programs" not out of love for the poor and oppressed but because the federal government refuses to allocate funds to them unless they at least appear to be doing something for black and brown people. The insidious thing about such programs is that they give our people the impression that because a few token Mexicans and blacks are allowed on campus, *raza* everywhere are somehow getting a break. And it is not so. The only thing such programs accomplish is that now, instead of one half of one percent, Chicanos represent one percent of the collegiate population. Even if this one percent advances 50,000 or 100,000 more of our people into the middle class, the rest of us (13 or 14 million in the Southwest) remain poor, illiterate, without jobs or social mobility.

The elementary and secondary schools continue to commit intellectual genocide against our children while the colleges and universities deceive our people into believing that progress is being made. Not only do they deceive us, they have co-opted some of the most promising potential leaders by turning many of the students into "tanned Anglos" or "assimilated" Mexican Americans who later move away from the *barrios*. But the Chicano movement on campus has shamed many of them into returning to their people; for *el que niega su raza ni madre tiene* (he who has denied his race, has denied his own mother).

Some of our people have started Chicano Freedom Schools to re-educate our children. Even if the public schools yield to the pressure we have been exerting on them and establish bilingual education programs for our children, Chicano Freedom Schools (like Corky Gonzáles's Tlaltelolco School in Denver) will be needed to supplement what the public schools are not equipped to do or do only in a distorted, Anglo way. "My children," says one Chicano father of three, "are bombarded with Anglo values for six and seven hours a day. Teachers don't just teach them the ABCs but how to believe in a way of life. I can see it affecting them. I can see the selfishness they've learned that day in school."

Chicano children must be educated as revolutionaries, which means that they must learn to read and write not because—as they are now taught by the public schools—they will then be able to go to college, get a good job, buy an expensive home, and take vacations in Europe. Our children must understand that reading and writing are skills to be learned so that they, in turn, can teach them to other poor Chicanos (fifty percent of them!) and so that together we can all use our intelligence in contributing to our new nation, Aztlán.

We are building Aztlán, and two potent weapons in our arsenal are confrontation and opposition. But the Chicano movement does not solely exist to criticize and condemn. We are creating a new order, a new humanity, first among ourselves and hopefully as an alternative that can be shared with all oppressed peoples. The central values of this new humanism are honesty and *carnalismo*.

. . .honesty can be contagious; it enables others to speak with equal honesty and candor. And if we make the effort to know ourselves, accept ourselves, and be ourselves, this is the basis of human cooperation, personal interaction, and community. For we are called to be honest not only with ourselves but with one another; we are called to be honest with the U.S. government and with Anglo society by making our feelings, our needs, our demands known.

The second value, *carnalismo*, is the social dimension and trust to personal self-awareness and honesty. We seek to know, accept, and be ourselves for the benefit and service of others. *Carnalismo*, roughly translated as fellowship and sharing brotherhood, means that we work alongside our *carnales* and *carnalas* as members of a *familia*.

Chicanos are fortunate enough to have a natural model for *carnalismo* because many of us have come from large families with relatives and *compadres* forming an extended *familia*. And even the *vatos* in the *barrios* who belong to gangs (the first gangs were formed to protect Mexican territory from foreign invaders) know what it is to depend on others not only for survival and protection but for fellowship as well. The movement has channeled many of the self-destructive tendencies of gang members into the struggle for Chicano liberation because *vatos* could easily comprehend and accept the *carnalismo* concept as applied to all of our people.

We are called to be fully human, fully Chicano, which means that each of us must put his *familia*, his *barrio*, his *raza* before himself. The best interests of *La Raza* come before any individual's comfort, wealth, or position.

Aztlán is being built on the personal sacrifices of Chicanos who say, "Mi Raza Primero!" (my people come first). They come before my selfish and individual plans or desires.

This nation has always existed in our hearts. And now we are building it with our hands on Mexican soil which has never ceased to be our own.

*In August 1972, members of the Brown Berets, a militant Chicano organization with over 90 chapters in the United States, invaded and occupied Santa Catalina Island, off the coast of California. Twenty-six Berets (including one woman) occupied a hill overlooking Avalon Harbor. According to Beret leader David Sánchez, the purpose of the occupation was to protest the illegal American "occupation" of land rightfully belonging to Mexicans. Authorities in Mexico as well as many Chicano groups in the United States claim that México never ceded the Channel Islands (which include Santa Catalina) to the United States at the end of the Mexican War. They point out that the Treaty of Guadalupe-Hidalgo makes no mention of the islands when describing the Mexican territory that would be annexed by the United States. The Berets renamed the island "Aztlán libre" (Free Aztlan) and stayed for twenty-four days until, surrounded by armed Sheriff's deputies, they were forced to return to the mainland. The Berets have vowed to return and are presently preparing for a second invasion. "Next time," says one Beret, "we'll bring the people of the *barrios* with us!"

ROLANDO R. HINOJOSA-S

MARCANDO TIEMPO

Aquí aparece gente que ya se ha visto en otras ocasiones; gente que apenas se ha mencionado y, todavía, otra gente que se conocerá. Este mundo de Belken County es un ir y venir: la gente que nace y grita también llora y ríe y va viviendo como puede; unos suben otros bajan pero, al fin, todos mueren y, al llegar la hora de la hora, aquí no ha pasado nada, señores: el muerto al pozo y el vivo al gozo, si se puede, y sin que lo cojan a uno con las manos en la masa.

El número de bolillos que se ve en estos escritos es bien poco. Los bolillos están, como quien dice, al margen de estos sucesos. A la raza de Belken, la gringada le viene ancha; por su parte, la gringada, claro es, como está en poder, hace caso a la raza cuando le conviene: elecciones, guerra, susto económico, etc. (Las cosas más vale decirse como son si no, no.)

Aquí no hay héroes de leyenda: esta gente va al escusado, estornuda, se limpia los mocos, cría familias, conoce lo que es morir con el ojo pelón, se cuartea con dificultad y (como madera verde) resiste rajarse. El que busque héroes de la proporción del Cid, pongamos por caso, que se vaya a la laguna de la leche.

Verdad es que hay distintos modos de ser heroico. Jalar día tras día y de aguantar a cuanto zonzo le caiga a uno enfrente no es cosa de risa. Entiéndase bien: el aguante tampoco es cerrar los ojos y hacerse pendejo.

La gente sospecha que el vivir es algo heroico en sí. Lo otro, lo de aguantar lo que la vida depare, también lo es. Saber mantener el tipo y no permitir que a uno se le aflojen las corvas también viene siendo, en gran parte, saber de qué se trata la vida. Lo demás (el sermoneo) es música de salón y ganas de chotear.

El aguante le podrá venir a uno de nacimiento. Todo puede ser. Pero por lo común, el aguante le viene a uno como consecuencia del forcejeo diario con el prójimo. No hay vuelta.

A continuación, *Generaciones y Semblanzas (entre diálogos y monólogos).*

LOS TAMEZ

A Jovita de Anda la preñó Joaquín, el mayor de los Tamez. En esos casos es difícil saber que va a pasar. . .

+ + + + + + + +

¡No, no, no y no! No anden con fregaderas.

Pero, papá, si la cosa. . .

Bertita, tú te callas, ¿sabes? Anda, vete alla al solar y déjanos.

Ahora tú, Emilio, ven acá.

Sí, apá.

Le avisas a don Manuel Guzmán que aquí no ha habido nada. No vayas a meter la pata, ¿me entiendes? Tú le dices que aquí va a haber paz y luego gloria; que aquí se van a casar esta tarde; y que por favor—y le dices *por favor,* ¿sabes?—que por favor apacigue a los de Anda.

¿Y eso paqué? ¿A poco van a venir aquí buscando a Jovita?

Estáte quieto, Joaquín. Emilio, haz lo que te digo. ¿Entiendes?

Sí, apá.

Cuélale. Ah. . .cuando vuelvas a casa te quedas allá afuera, al cruzar de la calle.

Sí, apá. Ahorita vuelvo.

Jovita.

Sí, señor.

Esa puerta allí es la del cuarto de mi difunta.

Sí, señor.

Enciérrate allí hasta que yo mismo venga a llamarte.

Sí, señor, sí.

Bueno, ahora ustedes dos vénganse conmigo al corredor.

+ + + + + + + +

Bonito lío hijuelachingada te has armado. ¿No te podías esperar, verdad? No, qué va—lo que digo yo: la rendija de la mujer estira más que un tractor.

Pero, apá.

Que apá ni que chingaos, Joaquín. Pendejeaste.

Pero usté sabe que nos queremos casar.

Sí—pero ¿por que chingaos no se esperaron a hacer la cosa bien hecha? ¿Y quién la va a pagar, eh? Pues, Bertita; sí, tu hermana. ¿Qué cara va a poner ahora con las amigas?

Ta bueno, apá.

Ah, hasta que habló el mudo. Milagro que no fuiste tú, Ernesto. Vas a ver, un buen día se le antoja a Cordero chico que le rondeas a la Marta y allí sí que va a haber pedo.

Balde me viene huango.

No te creas, Neto.

Joaquín tiene razón. Don Albino y yo somos viejos amigos. . .acuérdense que ellos también vivieron aquí en el Rebaje. El Balde es de esos que aguantan un chingo hasta que dan explosión. Entonces, ¡aguzaos! porque se pone buena la cosa.

No se crea, apá. Es un rajetas.

No es rajón, Ernesto. Es muy punto. Yo sé lo que te digo. No le menees.

Joaquín tiene razón, Neto.

Oiga, apá, ¿pero de veras no vamos a invitar a los de Anda?

¡Otra vez! Te dije que no, Joaquín. Que no, no y no. ¿Me entienden o no?

Pero, apá, es que Jovita. . .

Ni Jovita ni tú tienen vela en el entierro, ¿sabes? Ustedes se casan aquí, en esta casa, en ese cuarto donde murió tu mamá, ¿oíste? Que testigos ni que jodidos. Ernesto se trae al juez de paz y ya. El asunto del papelaje y todo lo demás se hace más tarde. . .y no me anden con chingaderas. Emilio va a estarse allá afuera, el juez y nosotros adentro, y tú y Jovita se casan.

¿Y si vienen los de Anda?

No vienen. El que quizá pueda venir es don Marcial pero el viejito no va a hacer mitote; lo conozco. Va a llorar de pena y rabia pero se va a aguantar y se aguantará.

Ya van a ser las dos, apá.

Ta bueno. Joaquín, vete a la puerta de atrás y dile a Bertita que entre. Díle que se quede con Jovita en el cuarto de tu mamá.

¿Y cuándo va Neto por el juez?

Vale más que ya. ¿Van a ser las dos, dices? Mira, Neto, no te vayas a detener por ningún lado, ¿me oyes? Te quiero ver aquí para antes de las tres.

¿Y si el juez no está en su casa?

Allí va a estar.

¿Pero si no está? ¿Entonces, qué?

Allí va a estar, te digo.

¿Y si no?

¿QUÉ PASA AQUÍ, CON UNA CHINGADA?

No se enoje, apá.

Mira, Neto, te aguanto mucho porque eres el más chico y porque le dije a Tula que me aguantaría—pero un buen día de estos te voy a dar una riatiza padre que no se te va a olvidar.

Ay, papá, ¿qué pasa?

No te metas, Bertita. Ándale. Al cuarto con Jovita.

Ya te estás yendo, Neto.

Sí, apá. Voy volado.

+ + + + + + + +

No es por nada, apá, pero usted le aguanta mucho a Neto. . .Que si Emilio o yo le habláramos a usté así ya nos hubiera puesto color de hormiga. Y Neto también tiene la culpa, apá. Es sangrón y aprovechado. Ya va más de una vez que lo hemos sacado Emilio y yo de zafarranchos, ¿y él? En las mismas. No se le quita.

Atiende, Joaquín. Esta casa y lo que tenemos es de todos.

Cuando yo muera, tú serás el encargado.

Sí, ya sé, el encargado.

Eso, el encargado. Ernesto sabrá arreglárselas por sí sólo, ya verás. Ahora tienes mujer y como eres el mayor tienes que cuidarte y vigilar a Bertita también. El día menos pensado cumple los dieciocho o diecinueve años y cuídate. Es tu hermana. El día que le dé la gana, se huye con alguien.

Quite usté, apá.

Yo sé lo que te digo. Tú la vigilas. . .No la queremos pá que se ponga a vestir santos, que chingaos, pero tampoco quiero que salga preñada.

Hombre, apá. . .no la friegue. . .lo va a oír Jovita.

Que me oiga—y que me oiga Bertita también. Lo de Jovita tiene arreglo: ustedes se casan en menos de una hora y ya. Se queda a vivir aquí y andando.

Fíjese por la ventana, apá. Allí está Emilio. ¿Lo llamo?

No. Ya sabes: vas a ser hombre casado y déjate de chingaderas. Eso es todo lo que te tengo que decir. Ahora llama a las muchachas y vamos a esperar al juez.

+ + + + + + +

Jovita de Anda y Joaquín Tamez se casaron tal y como había dispuesto don Salvador Tamez: boda pequeña y seria. De familia. Los de Anda, gente pacífica, la dejaron por la paz: Jovita estaba casada y que más se podía esperar. El suceso, claro, sirvió para dar parque a la gente del Rebaje y a la gente del Rincón del Diablo, dos barrios que a veces se llevaban bien y a veces no. Jovita, con el tiempo andando, sanó y se granjeó con su suegro al presentarle una mujercita a la cual le pusieron Gertrudis por nombre. Don Salvador Tamez, por su cuenta, siguió y sigue dando guerra a medio mundo.

Mucha gente (hasta la bolillada) dice que los Tamez son peleoneros y rascarrabias. Puede ser. Lo más probable es que no son dejados: saben cumplir a su manera, son mal sufridos y trabajan como animales.

plays

Vibiana Chamberlin
Teatro de los Niños

LAS ALBÓNDIGAS: A CHICANO CHILDREN'S PLAY

CAMPO SANTO

	(Spring music.)
Árbol de Vida:	(Stretches and scratches bark.)
	(Bird flies about árbol's branches and about cemetery crosses.)
Muertos:	(Hummmm. Stretch as they slowly rise from graves.)
Muerto 1:	Time for Spring cleaning. (Rearrange flowers. . . Switch them with Muerto 2.)
Muerto 2:	Hi, little worm! (Rearrange flowers. . . Put flowers on cross. . . sweep area)
Muerto 1:	Time to rest in peace.
Muerto 2:	Ummmmm, This feels cozy! (Wiggles into comfortable position.)
Muerto 1:	This sure is a good after-life.
Muerto 2:	Yeh! We have lots of privacy, lots of bird music and lots of flowers!
Árbol de Vida:	Yes. This life is good. Of course the seasons keep me very busy. After a long hot summer, all my leaves fall to the earth. The dirt is filled with my leaves. . . what a lovely place to be buried in. . . what a lovely place for worms to crawl in. . . what a lovely place for seeds to sprout in.
	Then Spring. . .Spring always comes. . . Leaves and flowers push out all over me. The birds build their nests on me. How lovely I become. I love being a tree.
Muerto 1:	Yes, I love being me too!
Muerto 2:	Me, too! I'm a very happy muerto!
Muerto 1:	But there are some people who aren't as fortunate as we are! I feel so sorry for them.
Muerto 2:	Yes we feel sooooo sorry for them! (Points to casita)

EL ZAPATO   CASITA

Niños:	We're hungry!
Niño 1:	I'm so hungry I can eat an hormiga!
Mamita:	Viejo. Go get us some liver. The kids are starving.
Viejo:	I have no money and no job. Where can I find some liver to buy?
Mamita:	Go out and try.
Niños:	Hurry daddy. Go get us some liver.
Niño 2:	¡Córrele, papá!

CAMPO SANTO

Viejo:	(Leaves house. . . Walks a long time and enters Campo Santo.)

Muertos:	Someone's coming!
Viejo:	(Respectfully takes boot off muerto 1.)
Muerto 1:	Hey you! Don't take my pretty zapato!
Muerto 2:	You've got a lot of nerve, viejo duro!
Viejo:	Thank you. (Leaves.)
Muertos:	You're not welcome!

CASITA

Viejo:	I'm home with the liver.
Niños:	Yeh! You found us some liver!
Mamita:	Liver! That looks like a zapato to me.
Viejo:	Cook it in water and it will taste delicious.
Mamita:	(She cooks zapato and serves it to the family.)
Niños:	Yumm. Delicious. ¡Qué Bueno!
	We're sleepy.
Mamita:	Let's go to bed now!
	(All sleep.)
Muerto 1:	Let's get my zapato!
Muerto 2:	Yeh. Let's scare that viejo duro!
Muertos:	Viejo, viejo duro. . . Dame mi dientes. (They haunt casita . . . Stomp feet.)
	Viejo, viejo duro. . . Da me mi zapato. (Repeat)
Mamita:	What is that? Viejo, wake up. What is that?
Viejo:	Go back to sleep, mamita. It's nothing.
	(He throws zapato out of the house.)
Muerto 1:	He'll never bother us again.
Muerto 2:	We sure scared him!

DIENTES POSTIZOS   CASITA

Familia:	(Awaken from night's sleep.)
Niños:	We're hungry!
Niño 2:	I'm so hungry I can eat a cucaracha!
Mamita:	Viejo, go get us some corn. The kids are starving.
Viejo:	I have no money and no job. Where can I find some corn to buy?
Mamita:	Go out and try.
Niños:	Hurry daddy. Go get us some corn.
Niño 2:	¡Córrele, papá!

CAMPO SANTO

Viejo:	(Leaves house. . . Walks a long time and enters Campo Santo)
Muerto 1:	Oh, no! He's coming again.
Muerto 2:	Hey, you, let us rest in peace! We should move somewhere else.
Viejo:	(Takes dientes from Muerto 2's mouth.)
Muerto 2:	Hey, Don't take my pretty white dientes away! (Talks mumbly without teeth)
Muerto 1:	You've got a lot of nerve!
Viejo:	Thank you very much.
Muertos:	You're not welcome!

CASITA

Viejo:	I'm home with the corn.
Niños:	Yeh! You found us some corn!
Mamita:	Corn! These look like false teeth to me.
Viejo:	Cook it in water and it will taste delicious.
Mamita:	(She cooks false teeth and serves them to the family)
Niños:	Yumm. Delicious. ¡Que Bueno! We're sleepy.
Mamita:	Let's go to bed now! (All sleep)
Muerto 1:	Let's get your dientes.
Muerto 2:	Yeh. Let's scare that viejo duro!
Muertos:	Viejo, viejo duro. . . Dame mi dientes. (They haunt casita . . . Clacky sound.) Viejo, viejo duro. . . Dame mi dientes. (Repeat)
Mamita:	What is that? Viejo, wake up. What is that?
Viejo:	Go back to sleep, mamita. It's nothing. (He throws dientes out of the house.)
Muerto 1:	He'll never bother us again.
Muerto 2:	We sure scared him!

LAS ALBÓNDIGAS   CASITA

Familia:	(Awaken from night's sleep.)
Niños:	We're hungry!
Niño 1:	I'm so hungry I can eat a mosca!
Mamita:	Viejo, go get us some albóndigas. The kids are starving.
Viejo:	I have no money and no job. Where can I find some albóndigas to buy?
Mamita:	Go out and try.
Niños:	Hurry daddy. Go get us some albóndigas.
Niño 2:	¡Córrele, papá!

CAMPO SANTO

Viejo:	(Leaves house. . . Walks a long time and enters Campo Santo.)
Muerto 1:	Oh no. He's coming again! He's coming again! We want peace. Leave us alone!
Muerto 2:	I'm turning my back to him!
Viejo:	(Respectfully takes tripas-albóndigas-from Muerto 1's stomach.)
Muerto 1:	Viejo duro, don't take my pretty albóndigas away! (Struggle.)
Muerto 2:	You've got a lot of nerve!
Viejo:	Thank you very much.
Muertos:	You're not welcome!

CASITA

Viejo:	I'm home with the albóndigas.
Niños:	Yeh! You found us some albóndigas!
Mamita:	Albóndigas! These look like tripas to me.

Viejo:	Cook it in water and it will taste delicious.
Mamita:	(She cooks the tripas and serves them to the family.)
Niños:	Yumm. Delicious. ¡Que Bueno! We're sleepy!
Mamita:	Let's go to bed now! (All sleep.)
Muerto 1:	Let's get my albóndigas.
Muerto 2:	Let's scare that old viejo duro!
Muertos:	Viejo, viejo duro. . . Dame mis albóndigas. (They haunt casita. . . Ooooooh sound.) Viejo, viejo duro. . . Dame mis albóndigas. (Repeat.)
Mamita:	What is that? Viejo, wake up. What is that?
Viejo:	Go back to sleep, mamita. It's nothing. (He throws albóndigas out of house. . . Muertos throw them back in house.)
Viejo:	(Tries to hand the albóndigas to muertos out of the house window.)
Muertos:	(Repeat chant.) Viejo, viejo duro. . . Dame mis albóndigas. (Ooooooh sounds.) Viejo, viejo duro. . . Dame mis albóndigas.
Viejo:	(He hands albóndigas through the front door of house. . .Muertos grab his hand and drag him out of the house.)
Muertos:	(Scare viejo with scary sounds. . . Drag him to the Campo Santo.)
Viejo:	(Rolls about; screams and cries.)
Muerto 1:	Why are you always bothering us?
Muerto 2:	Why do you take our pretty things away? (Shows audience dientes, zapato, albóndigas.)
Viejo:	My children are starving! I have no job and no money. I can't find food for my poor children. My children are starving!
Muerto 1:	Why didn't you tell us!
Muerto 2:	Yeh, We'll help you out!
Muerto 1:	Just show us some respect!
Muerto 2:	Tree of life, will you please give our friend some food. His children are starving.
Árbol de vida:	I'll be happy to help you out, viejo. I love to give my fruit away. Everyone is so nice to me. The wind and the rain help me all the time. And the birds sing to me all day long. I like to help everyone too! Have some fruit!
Viejo:	How can I thank you?
Muertos:	Come and bring us some flowers some time. Bring us some Marigolds.
Árbol de Vida:	Come and sing a song to us. We love music.
Viejo:	(Takes fruit to family.)
Mamita:	Where did you get these oranges?
Viejo:	From my friends. They invited us to a picnic.
Familia:	(Enter Campo Santo. . . Have picnic.)
Mamita:	Let's sing a song!
Unison:	Yo soy árbol—Yo soy árbol Yo soy viejo—Yo soy viejo Yo soy muerto—Yo soy muerto Todos somos unos. Unidos hermanitos. Unidos somos unos. Unidos arbolitos.

ESTRELLA DEL ORIENTE

estrella del oriente
que nos dió su santa luz
ya es hora que luchemos
por lo mero principal
por lo mero principal

queriendo ser dichoso
es el pueblo xicano
ya va abriendo y sembrando
la vereda roja
la vereda roja

el árbol de la vida
que nos dió su corazón
ya es hora que luchemos
por la tierra que da luz
por la tierra que da luz

la vereda roja
es la de amerindia
el sacrificio es el amor
para servir al pueblo

serpientes emplumadas
que nos dieron la misión
ya es hora que luchemos
por los pueblos que traen luz
por los pueblos que traen luz

queriendo ser dichoso
es el pueblo xicano
va ofreciendo y organizando
la mayor unión
la mayor unión

los gemelos sagrados
que nos dieron el valor
ya es hora que luchemos
y la tierra humanizar
y la tierra humanizar

la luz del quinto sol
está en nuestra presencia
obremos pa' servir al pueblo
hacia una gran conciencia

205

PASTORES EXCELSOS

pastores excelsos vamos a misión
pastoras excelsas vamos a misión
dichosos y ufanos
en la mera relación
en la mera relación

pastores excelsos vamos a misión
pastoras excelsas vamos a misión
surgiendo a la causa
de lo justo y necesario
de lo justo y necesario

pastores excelsos vamos a misión
pastoras excelsas vamos a misión
ubicando nuestro estudio
en nuestro corazón
en nuestro corazón

pastores excelsos vamos a misión
pastoras excelsas vamos a misión
generando la energía
terminando la opresión
terminando la opresión

pastores excelsos vamos a misión
pastoras excelsas vamos a misión
elevando nuestro espíritu
altísimo corazón
altísimo corazón

pastores excelsos vamos a misión
pastoras excelsas vamos a misión
religando a los pueblos
al tratado ascendiente
al tratado ascendiente

EL FLORÓN

el florón está en las manos
                está en las manos
en las manos del creador

el que me lo adivinaré
                divinaré
se le abre el corazón

¿la santa unión quién sembrará?
el que la siembre cosechará

la nación está en las manos
                'tá en las manos
en las manos del pueblo

el que me lo adivinaré
                divinaré
se le abre el corazón

¿liberación quién labrará?
el que la labre liberará

ALTISÍMO

altísimo corazón
que florezca

las razas en la nación
que florezcan

que florezca la luz
que florezca

la ciencia sin violencia
que florezca

el balance terrenal
que florezca

que florezca la luz
que florezca

altísimo corazón
que florezca

VAMOS CAMINANDO

vamos caminando hacia la vida real
hacia la vida real
vamos caminando hacia la vida real

vamos conociendo nuestra lucha ya
nuestra lucha ya
vamos conociendo nuestra lucha ya

corazón luciente estrella terrenal
trella terrenal
corazón luciente estrella terrenal

la luz en los rostros que ha de humanizar
que ha de humanizar
la luz en los rostros que ha de humanizar

la mortalidad que ya no ha de aquejar
que ya no ha de aquejar
la mortalidad que ya no ha de aquejar

vamos floreciendo sin fronteras ya
sin fronteras ya
vamos floreciendo sin fronteras ya

vamo' haciendo huelga por toda la nación
por toda la nación
vamo' haciendo huelga por toda la nación

NUESTRO SEÑOR QUETZALCÓATL

nuestro señor quetzalcóatl
ya se nos fue pa' los mares
en su barco de serpientes
se retiró pa'l oriente

todos los pueblos lloraron
pues los jaguares llegaron
hasta el hikuli se hizo agrio
pos los jaguares llegaron

pronto las bombas 'plotaron
y la guerra reanudaron
las flores se marchitaron
todos los ríos se secaron

todos los pueblos perdieron
el corazón inocente
el rostro de toda gente
perdió su luz ascendiente

ya las serpientes plumadas
con el árbol de la vida
muere la mata de espinas
dando su tuna y dulzura

brillan los rostros del pueblo
brotándoles energía
se hace la paz en la tierra
frutos de humana armonía

corazones colectivos
'ora nos toca rendirnos
para ganar nuestra gloria
se toma la decimplina

nuestro señor quetzalcóatl
ya regresó de los mares
en su barco de serpientes
ya retornó de los mares

CORRIDOR PROLETARIO

Aquí raza yo les traigo
el corrido proletario
el corrido de los pueblos
que son revolucionarios

el capitalismo yankee
oprime a todos los pueblos
a los pueblos de amerindia
los oprime y los subyuga

el proletaria'o xicano
se ha puesto ya en lucha firme
y la causa de los pueblos
es derribar el imperio

el imperio de los yankees
pronto ha deshumaniza'o
a los pueblos de colores
y a la tierra ha envenena'o

que se acaben ya las clases
que se mezclen ya las razas
que renazca la cultura
pueblos revolucionarios

CORAZÓN NOS CONOCEMOS

corazón nos conocemos
porque siempre hemos sido uno
ante nuestra madre tierra
ante nuestro padre sol

caminemos la vereda
del amor y el sacrificio
ascendientes nuestros pueblos
plantiando van l'amerindia

los valores pecuniarios
son valores en el viento
poruqe son convenencieros
derriban a nuestros pueblos

los valores de amerindia
son valores de la tierra
laborando con la vida
y gozando por la siembra

no le aflojen a la lucha
transformando l'energía
liberando la concencia
cultivando la materia

no negamos la energía
ni negamos la materia
por las dos en su dialética
nos entregan vida nueva

luchemos sin la violencia
pero con harta energía
ofrezcamos corazones
pero sin derramar sangre

SERVIDORES DEL ÁRBOL

servidores del árbol
de la santa y dulce vida
con encanto y energía
vámonos a hacer la lucha
vámonos a hacer la causa
vámonos, vámonos, vámonos, vámonos

trabajando con los pueblos
cultivando corazones
con amor sabiduría
vámonos a hacer la lucha
vámonos a hacer la causa
vámonos, vámonos, vámonos, vámonos

que se acaben ya las clases
que separan las naciones
que dividen a la tierra
vámonos a unir los pueblos
vámo'a a derribar imperios
vámonos, vámonos, vámonos, vámonos

generando justicencia
las cosechas que da'l árbol
son frutos humanizantes
vámonos a unir los pueblos
vámo'a derribar imperios

ACKNOWLEDGMENTS

ABELARDO. "At 26000 Feet," "Going Back to El Barrio," and "$," © copyright 1975 by Abelardo.

OSCAR ZETA ACOSTA. Excerpt from *Revolt of the Cockroach People,* © copyright 1973 by Oscar Zeta Acosta, reprinted by permission of the author.

TERESA PALOMO ACOSTA. "For Maximino Palomo," "Untitled," "Untitled," "For Santos Rodríguez," "Poema sobre Raúl," and "My Mother Pieced Quilts," © copyright 1975 by Teresa Palomo Acosta.

ALURISTA. "Sombras antiguas," "A oír raza," "Independencia y libertad," "La vida o la muerte," "A pelear," "Hacendado," "La paz," "Caminando van," "What it is/is/What it Does," "Mujeres de rebozo," "Nubes de lucha," and "Luna llena," © copyright 1975 by Alurista.

ESTEVAN ARELLANO. Excerpt from *Inocencio: Ni siembra ni escarda y siempre se come el mejor elote,* © copyright 1975 by Estevan Arellano.

RONALD ARIAS. "The Interview," © copyright 1975 by Ronald Arias.

TOMÁS ATENCIO. "La casa de aquélla," © copyright 1975 by Tomás Atencio.

MANUEL CARO. "You've Come Home," "To Willie," "Oh Mighty Soldier Where did you Stray?" "To Elena," "Untitled," "Were you There My Lord When They Crucified Us?" "If God had been a Faggot," "To Father Casey," and "My Dad," © copyright 1975 by Manuel Caro.

VIBIANA CHAMBERLIN. "Las albóndigas," © copyright 1975 by Vibiana Chamberlin, Teatro de los Niños

JUAN CONTRERAS. "Reflecciones hacia mi barrio," © copyright 1975 by Juan Contreras.

VERONICA CUNNINGHAM. "When all the yous," "Poor Animal," "I am Losing," "Love all you can," "Someday," "You Become Such," "Six Hours Later," "Always," "All the Winds," "Heaven Isn't Very Far," "Are we all so Fragile," "How can Your eyes," "Love," and "Why do I look," © copyright 1975 by Veronica Cunningham.

NEFTALÍ DE LEÓN. "No llevan flores," "Pulga (who wears a blue moon on her knee)," and "No No No," © copyright 1975 by Neftalí de León.

213

ENRIQUE LAMADRID. "The Hunt," "Up in a Lemon Tree," "Landmark," "Gabresto Lake," and "Petroglyphs of the Río Poñil del Norte," © copyright 1975 by Enrique Lamadrid.

E.A. MARES. "Far Away from Aztlán," "Spirit Song," "Reflections in the desert," "Landscape," "Juana la loca," "For Maria," "Seen and Overheard in a Chicano Bar," "On a Can of Coors Beer in a Chicano Bar," and "On Signing an Agreement to Read Poetry at a State University," © copyright 1975 by E.A. Mares.

JOSÉ M. MEDINA. "Sunny Afternoon," "Estoy en jardines," "Yo contemplo," "My Reflections," "Mirada de espinas," "Para soñar," "If You can see me," "Cuando yo no era nada," and "When I die," © copyright 1975 by José M. Medina.

JOSÉ MONTOYA. "Faces at the First Farmworkers Constitutional Convention," © copyright 1975 by José Montoya.

DORINDA MORENO. "Sounds of Sadness, Sounds of Sorrow, Sounds of Strength," © copyright 1975 by Dorinda Moreno.

ALEJANDRO MURGUÍA. "O California," "Canto del rojo y negro," "Sweet soledad," © copyright 1975 by Alejandro Murguía.

PRUDENCIO NAUNGAYAN. "El tecato," and "El estudiante y el tecato are one." © copyright 1975 by Prudencio Naungayan.

ANTONIO G. ORTIZ. "Sacramento," "October 1971," "Prism Prison" and "Macho," © copyright 1975 by Antonio G. Ortiz.

HENRY PACHECO. "In the Fields," "Listen-Those Words Come Into my Mind," and "I am Nothing but a Slight Brown Man," © copyright 1975 by Henry Pacheco.

JAVIER PACHECO. "Canto juvenil," and "Aztlán," © copyright 1975 by Javier Pacheco.

TOMÁS RIVERA. "Las salamandras," © copyright 1975 by Tomás Rivera.

LYNNE ROMERO. "Ola te saludo," "¿Por qué es que la gente que vive con la tierra ve al mar llorar?" "Instrument of Peace," "Speak Forth Fire Mouth," "Dejémonos deslizar," "Cuántas veces," "Cinco vidas," "To Sisters," "Nuestra liberación," © copyright 1975 by Lynne Romero.

OMAR SALINAS. "Quixotic Expectation," "Aztec Angel," "Sunday. . .Dig the Empty Sounds," "Ass," "Mexico Age Four," and "I am Omar," first appeared in

7021